MW01109575

"Inspiring, challenging, corrective and informational, all devotional and Biblical books should cover each of these, "The Gospel Of Matthew Through the Eyes of a Cop" by Sergeant Chuck Gilliland delivers each of these. Written by a cop for a cop, easy to read and easy to apply to everyday life, especially for those in Law Enforcement. I highly recommend this practical commentary on the book of Matthew".

-Lamar S. Moore, Executive Director Fellowship
of Christian Peace Officers-USA

"Chuck Gilliland believes that the Christian Peace Officer's ultimate purpose is to reflect the Jesus of the Bible in his or her passion to serve and protect! The Gospel of Matthew Through the Eyes of a Cop will point not only to the Cop, but anyone who understands the principles of Biblical authority, to live out this greater purpose everyday of their lives."

-Pastor Mike Fritscher, Senior Pastor
Cottonwood Baptist Church, Dublin Texas

"The Gospel of Matthew, Through the Eyes of a Cop...I am so thankful the Lord placed this vision on Chuck's heart! I am excited to see this book get into the hands of fellow brothers and sisters in blue. This walk through the Book of Matthew is a wonderful study for Officers, encouraging us of God's plan and grace, both at work and at home. Chuck brings to light the truths of Jesus' teaching in Matthew and shows us how to incorporate them in our daily life."

-Officer David B. Hornsby,
DFW International Airport DPS

"*Chuck Gilliland is a man of God first and foremost, but also a Police Officer with a heart for those who serve alongside him. One of the forgotten mission fields of the 21st Century is that of Law Enforcement. Chuck is providing a much needed resource for those of us in uniform. He has been sensitive to that need and it is exciting to see his insight, wisdom and spiritual depth shine through in this book. Chuck has been such a blessing in my life and I know that this book will be a tool that can be used to bless, challenge and disciple Police Officers.*"

–Sergeant Marvin Massacre, Woodstock Police Service, Ontario Canada, President Fellowship of Christian Peace Officers-Canada

"*Having been in Law Enforcement for almost 30 years and currently serving as an Officer, I can see the similarities and true parallels to this calling. I truly believe that these words should be placed in every Police Departments Rookie Book, so that every officer can see the Moral and Just Standards that every Police Officer should strive to live up to. Chuck is a great inspiration and example of Godly Moral Standards.*"

–Detective David B. Walters, Fort Worth PD, Secret Service, Former National Board of Directors FCPO

THE GOSPEL OF MATTHEW
Through the Eyes of a Cop

A Devotional for Law Enforcement Officers

CHARLES GILLILAND

CROSSBOOKS
PUBLISHERS

CrossBooks™
A Division of LifeWay
1663 Liberty Drive
Bloomington, IN 47403
www.crossbooks.com
Phone: 1-866-879-0502

©2012 Charles Gilliland. All rights reserved.

No part of this book may be reproduced, stored in a retrieval system, or
transmitted by any means without the written permission of the author.

First published by CrossBooks 07/03/2012

ISBN: 978-1-4627-1953-2 (sc)
ISBN: 978-1-4627-1955-6 (hc)
ISBN: 978-1-4627-1954-9 (e)

Library of Congress Control Number: 2012911238

Printed in the United States of America

This book is printed on acid-free paper.

Any people depicted in stock imagery provided by Thinkstock are models,
and such images are being used for illustrative purposes only.

Certain stock imagery © Thinkstock.

Because of the dynamic nature of the Internet, any web addresses or links contained in
this book may have changed since publication and may no longer be valid. The views
expressed in this work are solely those of the author and do not necessarily reflect the
views of the publisher, and the publisher hereby disclaims any responsibility for them.

CONTENTS

Micah 6:8 He has told you, O man, what is good; and what does the Lord require of you but to do justice, and to love kindness, and to walk humbly with your God?

FOREWORD

The law enforcement community is a tight-knit group, often times, to the exclusion of others. "Others" just don't understand who we are or what we go through. We tend to lean on other brothers or sisters in blue instead of those outside our community.

Charles Gilliland was born in Hico, Texas and grew up in Johnson County, just south of Fort Worth. "Chuck" loved listening to stories shared by his grandfather, who was a Texas State Trooper. These stories would later help shape his professional career.

Chuck attended Tarleton State University in Stephenville, where he met the love of his life, Angie. Chuck and Angie have two beautiful children and reside in Erath County.

Sgt. Gilliland has been an officer for over 22 years. He started working for Dallas PD, where he "cut his teeth" on police work in the South East District. From there, he moved to the Dallas Fort Worth International Airport Department of Public Safety where he was cross-trained for both police and fire. Sgt. Gilliland was the first bike officer at DFW and has been in a supervisor position for 12 years. Sgt. Gilliland is consistently nominated for supervisor of the year and always available for officers.

In 2005, Sgt. Gilliland felt a need to start a Bible study for officers at the airport. They began meeting at a local Starbucks and have met ever since. The Bible study group volunteers yearly with the Special

Olympics, hosts a blood drive and collects coats for a local homeless shelter.

Because Sgt. Gilliland has a heart to reach all police officers with the good news of Jesus Christ, he began a diligent study of the Book of Matthew. Through his study, and following the Lord's prompting, this devotional was born.

I highly recommend this book to you, my fellow brothers and sisters in blue.

God Bless You Big,
Officer D. Hornsby #844
DFW Int'l Airport DPS

PREFACE

The goal of this book is to teach the gospel of Matthew in a way law enforcement officers can see the need to put into practice, the lessons Jesus taught. Jesus calls each of us to live out our Christian walk when off duty and on duty. Most law enforcement officers don't live it out on duty. As you go through this book, you will see ways that you can put Jesus' teaching into practice.

The intent of this book is to serve as a devotional for law enforcement officers. I lead a weekly law enforcement Bible study in the Dallas/Fort Worth area. When I began writing, my purpose was to use these lessons in our group meetings. As our LEO Bible study group progressed through the material, I began to have the desire to see all LEOs have access to the studies.

I have assisted in helping several small LE groups start Bible studies. Questions I often get are:

    –Where do I get material to lead this group?
    –How do I set up a Bible study?
    –Do I need an outline or agenda?

This book takes The Gospel of Matthew and looks at it from the perspective of a LEO. The lesson starts out the same way a typical law enforcement agency would start their shift. The "briefing", simply put, is the process of passing information from the shift that is ending their tour of duty to the shift that is about to begin theirs. In this book, the briefing area will give you an idea of how to apply this lesson to your police duties. It may ask a question or have a short statement about how this lesson relates to law enforcement.

After the briefing, the "Dispatch (Assignment)" section will give the Bible verses for that lesson. Some lessons will also ask the reader to research other relevant information or ask a question.

Once the reading from Matthew is completed you will move to the "On the street" section. This is the meat of the study. For the individual reading of this book as a devotional, this is the main topic. For groups, this would be the area that would be the catalyst for discussion. Example: how does this lesson relate to your job? How can you take Jesus' teachings and apply them in your job? Can you use any of the principles learned from these passages?

The "Highlights from this read" is meant to be a mini commentary on the passage. It is intended to explain or shed light on the passage that may, or may not, have been discussed in "on the street". A small group leader can use this section to invite further discussion or questions.

As law enforcement officers, we are often performing follow up investigations. This section, "Investigation (Resources)", will provide other Bible references that relate to the passages from the study. A small group leader can have participants read the passages found in this section to reinforce points made in the study. I would also encourage the person reading this book as a personal devotion to follow up with these suggested reads.

The last section is titled "Officer Safety (Principles for the LEO to live by)". Law enforcement officers know that Officer Safety is paramount. The last section is also paramount. This section is intended to sum up the Bible study.

ACKNOWLEDGEMENTS

There are several people who helped me with the development of this study book. The first acknowledgement is my Lord and Savior. God gave me the inspiration, content and ability to write this book.

I had so much help from friends and family. I want to thank my wife Angie, who encouraged me, and my kids, Kate and Cole, who got really excited about the prospect of dad writing a book. Angie has been a spiritual compass in my life from the beginning. My grandmother loved Angie and before we got married she told me, "You and Angie are two completely different people, like two puzzle pieces that fit together perfectly". I can honestly say that being married to her has been the best 20+ years of my life. She is truly my other half.

Thank you to my dear friend and co-worker David Hornsby. David was a chaplain on the 1996 US Olympic team and a graduate of Tyndale Seminary in Fort Worth. He was my theological content review guy. Thanks David.

I want to thank my mother, Sandra Gilliland. She is a retired school teacher of 38 years. Mom was my proof reader. She pulled no punches and I would not want it any other way. I love you mom.

The Fellowship of Christian Peace Officers has been a huge influence on my life. People like Chuck Urgo, Sean Wallace, Mike Williams, Jim Hammond, John Stuermer, David Walters, Lamar Moore,

Mike Dye and Paul Lee. These guys are the spiritual giants in law enforcement.

Pastor Ron Horton, Pastor Mike Fritscher, and Pastor Dave Bollenbacher have been instrumental in my Christian walk and growth. God has used each of you to shape me. Thank you. Andrea Brandt, Derek Grace, Robert Mister, Chris Mea and Mike McKinney are cops who are Christians first. They live it and make no apology for it. You five constantly inspire me to be a better Christian cop.

One of the biggest influences on my early Christian journey was my grandmother, Laurian "Boots" Gilliland. She had a love for God's word that encourages me to this day.

Lastly I want to thank Jodie & Jeff, the owners of Beans & Franks. Their coffee shop is where I got some of my best work done. They provide a peaceful, Christian friendly environment that is so warm and welcoming. Jodie & Jeff, I'll see you Tuesday.

Thank you Jesus for your grace, love, patience and mercy on me, a sinner.

INTRODUCTION

I was 9 years old when I decided to follow Jesus. I had a great walk and journey with Christ right up to the day I entered college. While in college I put God on the back burner. I graduated Tarleton State University in 1990 and started my law enforcement career with Dallas PD soon after. After a couple of years I wound up at Dallas Fort Worth International Airport working for the Department of Public Safety as a cross trained fire fighter and police officer. I slowly began moving back into a relationship with God. I have been with DFW DPS for 20+ years, the last 12 as a sergeant.

God called me back to a deep personal relationship with Him in August of 2005. In August of 2008, my wife, Angie, and I went on a mission trip to Botswana. On our last day in Gaborone Botswana, I had a case of Bibles that I wanted to distribute to the police officers. I went to the Gaborone police headquarters and began giving out Bibles to officers in the break room. One officer asked me if I wanted to give Bibles to their supervisors and I gladly accepted. While I was handing Bibles to the Lieutenants and Captains I was swept into another office where I was presented to their detectives. As I was handing out Bibles to the detectives a Lieutenant came and told me that the Police Chief wanted to see me in his office. Not knowing what to make of this request, I prayed and followed the Lt. to the Chief's office. Once inside, introductions were made and the Chief invited me to come in and pray over him and his department. God opened doors that I could never gain access to on my own.

It was there that God made it very clear that he wanted me to serve in the mission field. I was surprised to find that He was not calling me to serve in Africa but to the culture of law enforcement. To reaffirm His calling and the scope of His intent, six months later I was asked to serve on the National Board of Directors for the Fellowship of Christian Peace Officers-USA. This book is further proof of His desire for me to continue to serve the men and women of law enforcement in their pursuit of a saving knowledge of Jesus Christ.

How to Use this Devotional

Briefing: Briefings are usually held at the beginning of each shift or tour of duty. The purpose of briefing is for the shift supervisor to pass information on to the officers coming on for duty. The information usually contains crime trends in patrol districts, suspect descriptions, areas that need extra patrols, and policy updates. Officers also get updated on upcoming events and other pertinent information.

Dispatch/Assignment: Police officers get calls and assignments from a dispatcher. This area is where you will find your assignment for the day.

On the Street: This is the first section of each chapter. It is where most police officers actually perform their jobs. This is where the rubber hits the road. "On the Street" is where you will find the meat of the devotional.

Highlights from this Read: This section includes a short commentary on the selected passage.

Investigation (Resources): As police officers, we often have to continue our investigations long after the call has ended. This is where you will find some suggested resources for continuing your study of the topic.

Officer Safety (Principles for the LEO to live by): For a law enforcement officer (LEO), officer safety is paramount. Police officers are taught their safety must come first. This can be a hard pill to swallow. Most people get into law enforcement with pure motives of helping people.

When you hear your safety comes before that of citizens', it can be a little confusing. Do not misinterpret what I am saying. Officers take this job knowing they put themselves between the general public and the evil of this world. We understand that we might lose our lives to save someone. That being said, if an officer gets a call of someone burglarizing a home, he or she cannot drive one hundred miles per hour to get there. We know the person who called expects us to get there as fast as we can, but the officer has to proceed in a safe manner. If they do drive with reckless abandon and have an accident on the way to the burglary, then they do the victim no good. As a matter of fact, the victim will not get the officer they needed in the timely response they expected because any other officer that might have come to their home will now be headed to aid the officer in need.

The goal of each "Officer Safety section" is to give officers the kind of information they need to keep them from falling into an unsafe area in life. We can avoid most pit falls if we just make each other aware of where they are.

Matthew 1

Briefing: One thing that all Law Enforcement has in common is the constant battle to maintain truth and justice. Truth is what Matthew was also about. He was out to prove to all Jews that Jesus was and is the Christ, the Messiah, God's son.

Dispatch/Assignment:
As you read this genealogy, see if you recognize any names. There is a broad mixture of people.

On the Street: Matthew marks the first time in 400 years since God had spoken to Israel. The Old Testament book of Malachi documents the last time God spoke through a prophet. Israel had forgotten what it was like to hear from God.

I would agree that most genealogies are boring. That's not the case with this one. It starts out by listing the patriarchs, Abraham, Isaac, and Jacob. In the middle of the genealogy we see that Jesus is a descendant of King David. That puts Him in line to be king. After the genealogy we get to the birth of Jesus.

Mary and Joseph were not the kind of people with which law enforcement usually deals. They were upstanding citizens. The Bible even calls them righteous and highly favored. That being said, Mary gets pregnant but not by Joseph. He had the right to stone her to death. Today this would be like citizens carrying out death penalties, vigilante justice.

The Bible calls Joseph, "A righteous man". We also learn that an angel of the Lord spoke to Joseph in a dream and he obeyed. As members of law enforcement agencies, we are in para-military organizations. We follow orders, but not from just anyone. We follow our chain of command. It is quite obvious to me that the angel of the Lord was in Joseph's chain of command.

Highlights from this Read: Jesus fulfills the prophecy that the Messiah would come from the seed of David. Joseph was not only Jesus' earthly/physical father but he was Jesus' legal father. Mary was also a descendant of King David. Her genealogy can be found in Luke. Either way you look at it, Jesus is a descendant of King David. In verse two we learn the line of Judah was blessed (Genesis 49:10). In verses 3-6 four women are mentioned; Tamar (Genesis 38), Ruth (book of Ruth) a gentile, Rahab (Joshua chapter 2) a gentile prostitute and Bathsheba (2 Samuel 11:12-25) an adulteress. The Holy Spirit wants us to see this genealogy and the people in it. It gives us hope that no one is beyond being used by God. Verses 2-15 lists "the father of" or "begat". These are all fathers and their children. In verse sixteen Joseph was not named "the father of" Jesus.

Investigation (Resources): Additional investigation can be done by reading Isaiah 42:1-9, 53:1-2, and 61:1-11. These passages predict Jesus birth and life. Luke 3:23-38 talks about Jesus' genealogy through His mother Mary. Matthew 1:19 Joseph is called righteous and in Luke 1:28 Mary is called "highly favored".

Officer Safety (Principles for the LEO to live by): Immanuel means God with us. Jesus was on this earth among His people. We can also have Him with us. As Christians, God is always with us. He is our permanent partner.

Matthew 2:1-12

Briefing: Do you follow anything? Sports, golf, hunting, a favorite team, a favorite show, or social media sites? Maybe you follow your kids and their extracurricular activities? Sometimes our hearts get captured by something and we find ourselves following "it" instead of pursuing God. What captures your attention?

Dispatch/Assignment: Read Matthew 2:1-12.

On the Street: Every time I read this story I am awestruck by the Magi. These guys showed up in Jerusalem after a two year journey. They'd followed a moving star. I wonder if they knew how long it would be before they reached the conclusion of their journey? Did they know what they would find when they arrived at the destination? The answer is yes. In verse two they asked King Herod, "Where is the one who has been born king of the Jews?" They were following hard after God.

When you set your mind to obtaining a goal, how long can you stay dedicated to achieving it? Do you get bored, impatient or distracted? For example, how many times have you set a goal to read the Bible? How far did you get? How bad did you want it? How dedicated were you?

Highlights from this Read: Bethlehem has an interesting meaning. It means "house of bread." The significance of this can be found in John 6:35, "Then Jesus declared, 'I am the bread of life. He who comes to me will never go hungry, and he who believes in me will never be thirsty.'"

In verse two, the star seems to have appeared to the "kings" in their country and led them on a two year journey to Jesus. In verse nine we see the action verbs "went" and "stopped" describing the star.

In verse eleven the Magi give Jesus three gifts. The first gift was gold. It was intended as gift for a king, symbolic of Christ's deity. The second was incense, which was used during prayer and symbolic of Jesus being our high priest. The third gift was myrrh, for His suffering and death. This was symbolic of Jesus being a prophet. Jesus was King, Priest, and Prophet. This is a fulfillment of Hebrews chapter seven.

Investigation (Resources): Micah 5:2 is fulfilled in Matthew 2:6. Luke 2:1-20 is the other Gospel account of Jesus' birth.

Officer Safety (Principles for the LEO to live by): Search hard for an intimate relationship with Jesus. We should pursue Christ like some people follow their favorite sports team. Let's get fanatical!

Matthew 2:13-23

Briefing: Have you ever been asked to do something as a LEO that you did not think was right? Have you ever participated in conduct that you knew was wrong? Are you old enough to remember the Rodney King incident? I was a rookie at the Dallas Police Academy when this happened. I remember an instructor asking me if I would have had the courage to do the right thing.

Dispatch/Assignment:
Read Matthew chapter 2:13-23.

On the Street: Don't get me wrong, Rodney King was a criminal and was a danger to officers that night but were the officer's actions excessive? The video tape shows Officer Briseno moving in to try and stop Officer Powell. Even Sergeant Koon, at one point yelled, "that's enough".

I can't help but think of the police force that served under King Herod. How would you react to the order to go and kill children? What's the job worth to you? Could you stand up and say, "NO"? This is not an easy question or lesson but being a Christian is not easy. Jesus said, "take up your cross and follow me".

Highlights from this Read: In verse fifteen we have an example of Matthew proving, through prophecy, that Jesus is the promised Messiah. This passage can be found in Hosea 11:1.

In verse 16 we see Herod make the call to kill all the children two years old and younger. The reason was that Herod was not sure exactly how old the King was so, to be safe, he ordered all infants two and younger to be executed.

Verse seventeen is a fulfillment of Jeremiah 31:15. This is just more proof that Jesus is the Messiah.

Rachel was Jacob's wife and the grandmother of Ephraim and Manasseh. Ephraim and Manasseh were the most powerful tribes of Israel and used to personify the whole nation. This can be found in Genesis 29-30

Joseph was afraid to go back to Judea when he heard that Archelaus was ruling. Archelaus was an evil person. He condemned 3000 people to death and had them killed during Passover.

Investigation (Resources): The more traditional Christmas story is found in Luke 2. Additional investigation: Nazarene (verse twenty-three) in Hebrew means shoot/branch. Look up passages on branch in Isaiah 4:2, Jeremiah 23:5, Zechariah 3:8, and 6:12.

Officer Safety (Principles for the LEO to live by): As a Christian Peace Officer you will be looked at by law enforcement officers who are not Christians. They will judge what you do or don't do and label it Christianity. We have an awesome responsibility, one that we will never be able to justify. We will never be perfect but we are on a journey toward that goal. Integrity counts as a law enforcement officer and more importantly as a Christian law enforcement officer.

Matthew 3

Dispatch/Assignment:
Read Matthew chapter 3.

Briefing: I don't know a lot of LEOs who garden or farm but in Jesus' day everybody farmed. Fruit and producing fruit is a recurring theme in the Bible and something you will see often. You don't have to be a farmer to produce fruit in your life.

On the Street: God and Israel were going in opposite directions. John's purpose was to bring them back into relationship. Amos 3:3, "Do two walk together unless they have agreed to do so?" Israel needed to repent. John makes a statement here that we need to ask ourselves. He says, "produce fruit in keeping with repentance". Are you producing fruit in keeping with repentance? In other words, are you living your life in a way that others can see you making changes to your life and show you walking on the correct path.

Airplanes have gauges that keep them on a true path. Arrows have fletching to keep their flight straight. Scopes have adjustment knobs that can be adjusted for windage and elevation. As an LEO I also have an integrity check for a true path. Whenever I come across a situation where I am confused or distracted and I find myself off the true path I ask myself, "Is this legal, is it moral, and is it ethical". The answer to these questions will steer me back on the correct path.

As a Christian I also have checks and balances to gauge where I am on my Christian walk. Am I producing fruit in my life? The kind of fruit John is talking about can be found in Galatians 5:22-23.

<u>Highlights from this Read:</u> In verse three, "make straight paths for Him" comes from Isaiah 40:3.

In verse nine there is a reference to Abraham's children. The Jews believed that by being a descendant of Abraham, their salvation was already secure. They believed they were saved by virtue of their family tree (John 8:31-59 shows more of this attitude).

Verse ten says the axe is ALREADY at the root. It has already been brought from the shed and laid next to the tree to use. This is your last chance.

In verses eleven through twelve, John is foretelling Jesus' second coming but he doesn't realize it. There are two baptisms, the first is the baptism with the Holy Spirit. This is the first coming of Christ. The baptism with fire will be Jesus' second coming. John, like many Old Testament prophets (Daniel, Isaiah, and Ezekiel) did not see this as two separate events. (Matthew 11:2-3). Holy Spirit baptism is found in Acts 1:5-8.

We see John, in verse thirteen, wants to be baptized with the Holy Spirit by Jesus. Realize that in verse fifteen Jesus is being baptized in obedience to His Father, not for sin. As the baptism comes together in verse seventeen we see the Holy Trinity together (Father, Son and Holy Ghost). Isaiah 42:1 and Psalm 2:7 speak of Jesus' family showing up like they did at His baptism.

<u>Investigation (Resources):</u> James 2:14-26 shows us the difference between faith and deeds. See Mark 1:3-8 and Luke 3:2-17 for companion stories.

<u>Officer Safety (Principles for the LEO to live by):</u> Are you producing fruit in keeping with repentance? When was the last time you confessed your sin to God and asked for forgiveness?

Matthew 4:1-11

Briefing: This appears to be a training mission. Was there a time in your career where you were faced with a temptation that seemed to be made specifically for you? It was as if the person tempting you knew exactly what your weakness was.

Dispatch/Assignment:
Read Matthew 4:1-11. What kind of temptations did Jesus face and how did He handle them?

On the Street: As a Christian have you ever been told that there are different kinds of temptation? There are temptations that we are expected to fight through then there are those that we are told to flee from. Part of the battle for Christians is being able to recognize what kind of temptation you are facing and then how to handle it.

Let's put it into an example that we can relate to. Say you get dispatched to a call for service. After you get the call and are in route to the location, you start running scenarios through your mind. If this call is X then it is a civil matter, if it turns out to be Y then it is a criminal matter.

Sometimes we confuse temptation with God's testing. We are to persevere through His testing of us because it is given to us as an opportunity to succeed and please Him. We are to flee from temptation (James 1:13).

As LEOs, we are trained to be fluid and react appropriately depending on the situation. Every traffic stop is not the same. This is a fundamental part of Officer Safety. Why don't we train new Christians with the same techniques?

Highlights from the Read: This is such a rich story. In the first verse we see that Jesus is led into the desert by the Holy Spirit. This is a test. In verse two, Jesus is hungry. I have often heard it said that we are most vulnerable to temptation when we are hungry, tired, or lonely. In my own life I have proven this to be true time after time.

Have you ever been in a situation where you are performing your official duties and the person you are talking to decides to explain the law to you? I think it is interesting that Satan tries to trip Jesus up by using scripture. Jesus wrote the scripture! (John 1:1)

The last verse in this lesson is eleven. Luke's account says something that we all need to take note of, "*When the devil had finished all this tempting, he left Him until an opportune time.*" Luke 4:13.

Investigation (Resources): Here are some other places in the Bible to study about temptation. James 1:12-16, 1 Peter 1:3-8, 1 Corinthians 1:12, 6:18, 10:14, 1 Timothy 6:11, and 2 Timothy 2:22. Mark 1:12-13 and Luke 4:1-13 are companion stories.

Officer Safety (Principles for the LEO to live by): It's not a sin to be tempted, Jesus was tempted. It's how we handle the temptation that determines if you have sinned or not.

Matthew 4:12-17

Briefing: Police work can be a dark place. I was a cop for fifteen years before I boldly confessed Christ to my fellow officers. I was amazed at how many of them admitted to being Christians also. Why didn't we know this about each other until now?

Dispatch/Assignment:
Read Matthew 4:12-17. How bright, or dull, is the light in your agency?

On the Street: I learned to be a police officer in the mean streets of South East Dallas. You could categorize it as "the land of the shadow of death". You had to be tough or you would get your rear end handed to you by the people who lived there. I learned real fast, contrary to what I had been taught growing up, most people only responded to you if you spoke their language. I had to learn the language.

The officers I worked with were just as hardened and tough as the people who lived in my district. I couldn't talk about Jesus with these guys they would think I was weak. Unfortunately this became a theme in my life at work. I changed jobs, moving to another police department where I realized that the environment changed but officer's attitudes didn't. At that time I did not care, I had a reputation to uphold after all I was a tough cop from South Dallas. I hope this story does not mirror your own career.

In these verses we see that Jesus fulfills a prophecy out of Isaiah 9:1, "The people walking in darkness have seen a great light; on those living in the land of the shadow of death a light has dawned." Do you work in darkness, the land of the shadow of death? There is good news for us that do, Jesus is the great Light and the light has dawned.

Highlights from the Read: Jesus set up His base of operation in Capernaum. He traveled in and out of this city. Keep this in mind because we will revisit Capernaum and the law enforcement officers who live there. Capernaum was a city that sat on a major trade route. This was important because of the volume of people that would encounter Jesus then return to their home, spreading the news of Him and His gospel.

Another recurrent theme is proof. Here Matthew proves again that Jesus is the Messiah.

Investigation (Resources): Isaiah 9:1-7 is a great prophecy of Jesus' life. I highly suggest that you read the entire book of Isaiah specifically looking for Jesus in every verse.

I'm getting a little ahead of myself but Matthew 5:13-16 is an awesome section that speaks directly to our call to be salt and light in this dark world. Also see John 1:9

Officer Safety (Principles for the LEO to live by): Don't miss the opportunity to be the light that your fellow employees need. Be the salt and light that God has called you to be.

Matthew 4:18-25

Briefing: Imagine Jesus is walking through your jurisdiction. You have heard of Him, you may have even heard Him speak. As He is walking by He looks directly at you and says, "Come follow me". What would you do?

Dispatch/Assignment:
Read Matthew 4:18-25.

On the Street: Growing up I always had a fear that God was going to call me to be a missionary. I cringed at the thought of having to live in a mud hut in Africa.

Here we see Jesus recruiting missionaries. He is not asking them to go to Africa or China He is asking them to serve in their own country. Jesus walks into our jurisdiction and tells us to come with Him. "I will make you fishers of men". As a police officer, I can relate to this statement. I used to "fish" for drunk drivers. You know, go to your favorite hole where the chances of catching your favorite prey are really good, someplace where you have had success in the past.

Jesus calls us to be fishers of men right where we are. Have you been casting your net, or line, in your pond? We all have a sphere of influence, people who we hang out with, work with, family, and friends. As a law enforcement officer we are in a particularly rich environment. We see people at their worst. This is the time when they need Christ the most! The fish are jumping, is your line in the water?

<u>Highlights from the Read:</u> In verse twenty-two it describes their response as, "immediately". This needs to be our response (Luke 9:59-62).

James and John were part of Jesus' inner circle (Matthew 17:1, Mark 5:37 and Mark 14:33-40). We will see this again as we move through Matthew.

Verses twenty-three through twenty-five sums up Jesus' ministry. Here we see Him teaching, preaching and healing. As long as He was healing the physical ailments and meeting the physical needs of the crowd, they followed Him. These people flocked to Him for physical healing.

In verse eighteen, Jesus called Andrew. Jesus had met him before, see John 1:39.

<u>Investigation (Resources):</u> In the Old Testament the idea of being a fisher of men would not have been a good thing. It usually meant judgment as seen in Jeremiah 16:14-16 and Amos 4:2.

You can also read about Jesus calling the disciples to "fish for men" in Mark 1:16-20, Luke 5:2-11 and John 1:35-42.

<u>Officer Safety (Principles for the LEO to live by):</u> Obey the call of Jesus. He is not going to call you to anything that He has not already prepared you to do. Can you imagine Jesus telling you, "Come follow me, I'll make you fisher of LEOs"?

Matthew 5:1-12

Briefing: Does your department have a code of conduct? Do you work for an agency that has policies and procedures that have nicknames like, the "Chuck" rule (these are policies written because of the actions of a single person). Because man is sinful, human civilizations have had to make rules to govern our behavior.

Dispatch/Assignment:
Read Matthew 5:1-12 then write down, in your own words, what the Beatitudes mean to you.

On the Street: In these verses Jesus is not giving us a new law. Laws provide negative consequences for unacceptable behavior. In part, they are a deterrent. What Jesus is giving us is the opposite of law these are blessings for behaviors that please God.

An interesting thing about the Beatitudes is the fact that they are a mirror image of the Christian life as it progresses in maturity. Jesus blesses the poor in spirit as they humble themselves and cry out to God to save them. He blesses those who mourn over their own sin, making a complete one hundred and eighty degree change in behavior (repenting). He blesses those who are self controlled and those who strive to know God's word.

Blessed are the merciful for they will be shown mercy. This is a great independent study. Search your Bible for mirrored verses. For example, Jesus said that God will forgive those who forgive their brothers but He will not forgive those who do not forgive their brothers.

Jesus blesses the pure in heart, the peacemakers and those who are persecuted because of righteousness. Lastly, He saves the greatest blessing for those who are insulted, persecuted and lied against because of the stand they take for Christ.

<u>Highlights from the Read:</u> What would this profession look like if we taught the Beatitudes in Police Academies? LEOs are expected to have integrity, honor, be courageous and be truthful. There is not a better guide for these characteristics than the Bible! Verse three tells us to be humble (strength under control). Verse four teaches us not to be prideful and arrogant. How many times has your pride written a check that you could not cash? In verse five we learn to be righteous by clean living. We see in verse six that we should seek God's truth and apply it in our lives. Verse seven tells us to be merciful and we will receive mercy. I was never taught that. I was told to kick butt and take names. Verse eight says to have a pure heart, integrity and character. How refreshing! Verse nine is a lesson all unto itself. Be a peacemaker. Not just a peace officer but a peacemaker. Ten tells us to stand up for what is right. Isn't this our calling as law enforcement officers? Lastly we are told to love Jesus and follow His example. He is the greatest leader of all time. ALL TIME!!! How many other people do you know that have time marked by their birth and death?

<u>Investigation (Resources):</u> Galatians 5:22-23 is the list of the Fruits of the Spirit. This is another list of Christian characteristics we should learn from and utilize. Luke includes this teaching in his version found in Luke 6:20-23.

<u>Officer Safety (Principles for the LEO to live by):</u> Memorize the Beatitudes. Many officers will memorize phonetic alphabets, 10 codes, exact chapter and verses of law, and Miranda warnings. How many scriptures do you know? The Beatitudes are a great place to start.

Matthew 5:13-16

Briefing: As I read these verses I see a large neon sign that says, "This applies to law enforcement officers on the job as well!" As you read it, see if you get the same application.

Dispatch/Assignment:
Read Matthew 5:13–16 and think about your calling as a police officer. Are you a light in your world?

On the Street: Did you know that salt was used to pack meat before the advent of refrigeration? People used salt as a preservative. They would pack meat in salt to keep it from rotting. We are called to be the substance in this world that keeps it from rotting. That sounds like something very specific to law enforcement.

Jesus takes it a step further and says, "You are the light of the world". I love this statement and the implications it has for law enforcement. Bad guys love the dark. They can hide in the shadows. As a child I knew that monsters only came out at night. As a twenty year police officer, I am more convinced than ever that monsters come out at night. Besides guns, what piece of equipment do police spend the most money on? Answer: Flashlights. Why? Answer: to expose darkness.

We are to be the reflection of Christ's light. We need to be the kind of Christian cops that light the path to officers who are lost and in the dark.

You are called to be salt and light. This calling is so much more than just being a good cop with integrity. You were called to lead your fellow brothers and sisters, in law enforcement, to Christ. I can't think of a better way to sum this up than what Jesus said, "…let your light shine before men, that they may see your good deeds and praise your Father in heaven." AMEN!

Highlights from the Read: In verse thirteen Jesus starts by saying, "You". Do you have any doubt that He was talking directly to us? I can almost see Him looking at me; kneeling down like a father who is about to teach his young son how to catch a baseball. You can see the look of excitement and expectation in His eyes. "You have greatness in you, I can see it", He explains.

Salt is different from the foods it is added to for flavor. When a Christian stops being different from the world and no longer works against the forces of decay, that person stops being salt to the earth. Such a Christian will have no positive influence in the world. It is the same for a LEO. You, LEO, are the thin blue line between chaos and civility, but if a LEO loses his/her integrity, how can they be trusted again? They are no longer good for keeping the peace. They have crossed to the other side of the thin blue line and have become the enemy.

Investigation (Resources): We read in Leviticus 2:13 how we are to add salt to all of our offerings. If you read John chapter one you will see that Jesus is the true light.

Officer Safety (Principles for the LEO to live by): You have a calling to be salt and light to those around you. The consequences of losing your saltiness are not good.

Matthew 5:17-20

Briefing: One of the things I take great comfort in knowing is God is the same today as He was yesterday and will be tomorrow. I like that rock solid assurance. What else can you think of that you can trust in to be there no matter what?

Dispatch/Assignment:
Read Matthew 5:17-20. It might also be interesting to compare departmental policy on a topic, car chases for example, to see how it has changed in the last couple of years.

On the Street: As LEOs, one thing we rely on is the law. The thing about earthly law, whether it is federal, state, local or departmental law is; it often changes. I have worked for an agency where the administrators would change policy and/or procedure at will. There were periods of time when I would walk into work and have to ask what the policy was for that day.

Jesus reassures the crowd that He has not come to "abolish" the law. He has come to rock their world and correct their misunderstanding of the law. They, like us, have gotten confused on what He has called us to be. We get so wrapped up in man-made laws, and following it "to the tee" that we miss the purpose and the intent.

Jesus speaks of fulfilling the law. How? All the prophecies that were written are coming true in Him. He has come to be a living example of how we are to live. He is the fulfillment of the law.

When you are off duty, are you the fulfillment of the law? Do you speed, run red lights, lie, look lustfully at another person, or have anger towards someone? The word Christian was originally a put down to people who imitated Jesus. They were called "little Christ's". Now we proudly wear it like a badge!?! Don't we? We are called to walk around teaching and telling others about Him. Your actions speak louder than your words! Do you lead by example?

Highlights from this Read: "unless your righteousness surpasses that of the Pharisees and the teachers of the law, you will certainly not enter the kingdom of heaven". Wow, that is scary. This is not some insurmountable, impossible feat. The righteousness of the Pharisees and the teachers of the law were works without faith. The Pharisees of Jesus' time were not very righteous; therefore, this was something that could be accomplished with a little work.

Investigation (Resources): For more on faith and works see James 2:14–26.

Officer Safety (Principles for the LEO to live by): When you are off duty, how is your behavior? Are you setting the example? If Jesus was the sun and you were the moon, how much of His light would you be reflecting to others around you?

Matthew 5:21-30

Briefing: Have you ever arrested a murderer before? Have you ever arrested someone for minor theft? In your experience, what is the difference between these two law breakers?

Dispatch/Assignment:
What definition does your agency or jurisdiction use for murder? What is the required culpable mental state? Read Matthew 5:21-30.

On the Street: When I was still in training, I arrested my first murderer. There was nothing glamorous about it. It did not meet the expectations set by watching too many cop shows and movies. She was a drug addict that killed the owner of a bar. It never made the news. I didn't get any awards or recognition, just a lot of paperwork. The reason I bring this up is, although I may not have gotten any awards, I made sure all of my friends and family knew about it. Some years later I found my notes from that day. It seems that I made another arrest that day. At the beginning of my shift, I arrested a shoplifter. It was so uneventful that I have no recollection of it today.

Do you believe that murder is a sin, the same as theft is a sin? Do you believe that lying is a sin? Do you believe that sin is sin no matter what "degree" or "class" it is? I have a hard time wrapping my brain around this because I was trained to classify sin into misdemeanors and felonies. Then, we break them down into smaller penalty classes so each sin is judged according to its severity.

When I read this passage, I get the feeling that Jesus is telling me, "sin is sin". The sin of anger that I committed today because someone cut me off in traffic is just as black and white as the murderer I arrested over twenty years ago. Sin is black and white, you either commit sin or you don't. This is a sobering thought. It really puts into perspective just how much I need God's grace and mercy and the importance of His forgiveness.

Highlights from this Read: In verse twenty-one we see the phrase, "Do not murder". I'm sure you recognize this from the Ten Commandments. Growing up I was taught that the commandment was do not kill. The true translation is murder. As a LEO, this is very important for our line of work.

Verses twenty-three through twenty-four, paint a clear picture for us. They tell us to never leave our anger unattended. We must face it and fix it. See more on this topic in the Investigational Resources.

For verses twenty-five and twenty-six, there is a great illustration found in Matthew 18:21-35.

Investigation (Resources): For more on dealing with anger see Ephesians 4:26 and Matthew 18:21-35. The study on Matthew 19:1-12 is much more in-depth on divorce. Also, see Luke 12:58-59.

Officer Safety (Principles for the LEO to live by): As LEOs we sometimes get into the habit of seeing everyone else's sin as worse than ours. We sometimes see the worst that society has to offer and the worst in humanity. Stay humble and accept how much you need God's grace and mercy. Pray for it.

Matthew 5:33-37

Briefing: LEOs can be a crude, rude, socially unacceptable group. If you are surprised by this, then I am glad. I have been around LEOs most of my life and I can tell you from my experience that we can make sailors blush.

Dispatch/Assignment:
Make two lists of curse words. The first list should be words that are considered acceptable and the second list should be the really bad words. These are the words that if your mother heard you say them she would wash your mouth out with soap.

On the Street: Have you ever taken an oath? If you are a LEO then the answer to this question is yes. We take oaths when we receive our commission or warrant of appointment. Some of us even have to testify in court which requires an oath to tell the truth.

In Jesus' time people also took oaths. They would use an oath to swear. Oaths that made use of God's name were considered binding. For fear of not being able to keep a promise, a person might swear by something less than God's name, Jerusalem or earth. Jesus totally rejected this practice.

Jesus tells us not to swear by anything. Not only that, but He tells us not to use any expletives. Jesus says that it is not the column that the word comes from but the intent in which you use it. I could call someone a socially unacceptable name or a jerk. The word is not the issue. The issue is the amount of hate and anger in my heart that I am venting towards a person.

Jesus says in verse thirty-seven, "Simply let your yes be yes and your no, no, anything beyond this comes from the evil one." Jesus puts forth a simple truth, if you always tell the truth you never have to use oaths to convince anyone that you are speaking the truth.

<u>Highlights from this Read:</u> Oaths, in this instance, seem to be prideful arrogant speech. There is power in the spoken word as explained in James chapter three. The tongue has the power of life and death in it.

Numbers 30:1-2 says that God holds us to the vows we make to Him. We better be sure we can keep our word.

Verse thirty-seven says, "anything else". That means any slang words or expressions of disgust. I am guilty of this.

<u>Investigation (Resources):</u> To read more about what Jesus says about our speech read Matthew 12:24 and 15:1-20.

<u>Officer Safety (Principles for the LEO to live by):</u> Don't let your language be a stumbling block to other officers. If you have a problem conquering your speech just take small steps and work to improve day by day.

Matthew 5:38-48

Briefing: Have you ever been involved in a call where you had to deal with an individual that was so evil that the anger and/or hatred of him/her stayed with you long after your shift ended? Anytime I have to deal with individuals who victimize children I get really ugly, negative feelings towards the suspect.

Dispatch/Assignment:
Read Matthew 5:38-48.

On the Street: This is one of those lessons where we find out if we can truly put into practice the things God has called us to do.

How many times have you wanted to practice the "old saying", an eye for an eye and a tooth for a tooth? I know I have. This is a natural human instinct but as a LEO we are called to rise above this kind of thinking. This is what the "thin blue line" is all about. When others want to act on their impulse for vengeance, we have to be self-controlled so that justice can be carried out. There have been several times in my career that I wanted to cross the line but didn't.

As a LEO I stand as the thin blue line that separates chaos from civility. It is the same in our Christian life. We are called to be different. While we are here we assist the Holy Spirit in keeping the man of lawlessness away. (2 Thessalonians 2:1-12)

Another question for you; How do you feel about homeless people begging you for money or giving you a pencil and asking you to donate money for it? Jesus addresses this in verse 42 when He says to give it to them. Don't worry about them trying to scam you, don't make it about YOU. Do it out of obedience to HIM. Do it because you love Him and want to please Him. Put into practice the things Jesus has commanded us to do.

Lastly, how hard is it to love the person you arrest, who hates your guts and spits on you when they get the chance? How hard is it to love the citizen who complains on you for driving too fast, not knowing you are going to a dangerous call to help someone. How hard is it to love the reporter who calls you a Nazi or Storm trooper with a heavy badge? This is why Jesus calls us. We are called to be set apart, to be different from the world, not to look like the world but to contrast it.

It was a hard lesson for me to learn. One day in a Sunday school class I was asked to picture in my mind the person I hated the most in this world. That was easy. Next I was given a piece of paper folded, told to draw a stick figure on it and to write down the person's name. I was enjoying this. Next, the drawing (stick figure) of the object of my animosity was put on a wall and I was handed three darts. I was told to throw the darts at the drawing. After I put three beautiful holes in my stick figure, the teacher of the class gave me the picture and told me to unfold the paper. As I unfolded it, on the inside was a picture of Jesus. As you guessed, I had put three holes in my savior. It was a lesson that will never depart from me.

Investigation (Resources): To find out more about the man of lawlessness read 2 Thessalonians 2:1-12.

Officer Safety (Principles for the LEO to live by): If you have been on the job for long you know how it feels to have a hardened heart. This is a defense mechanism for people who have to deal with ugly, unpleasant situations on a regular basis. This is very dangerous for anyone and can prevent us from acting out the love that we are called to by Jesus. Guard against hardening your heart.

Matthew 6:1-18

Briefing: Do you wear a uniform at work? For those of us who do, some departments have awards programs that award officers with ribbons that you wear on your uniform. Some military people call them salad bars. If you do, you may understand the importance of having a few ribbons so people don't think you're a rookie.

Dispatch/Assignment:
Read Matthew 6:1-16 and see if you can see yourself in this passage; I can.

On the Street: Napoleon Bonaparte said, "Give me enough shiny pieces of clothe, and I can rule the world". How sad!

I can remember the day I got my first ribbon for my uniform shirt. It was white with two black bars running vertically. It was a marksmanship bar. To receive this award you had to shoot ninety eight or better at three consecutive pistol qualifications. I wore it proudly. It proved to the world that I was no longer a ribbonless rookie. I didn't wear it because of the achievement. No, I wore it for other officers to see. At one point in my career it became my goal to be the most decorated officer in the department. My aim was not to be the best public servant, it was to fill my chest with ribbons so everyone could see how important I was. I was already a legend in my own mind, I just needed to convince everyone else that I was Super Cop.

Jesus addresses this issue head on. He tells us that we are not to live to please other men but to please our heavenly Father. He goes so far as to tell us to do these things in secret. Jesus is talking about a genuine attitude of generosity and service.

I don't know about you, but I feel I was called to this profession. When I got hired, my goal was to help people. I truly wanted to protect and serve. Somewhere this noble goal got twisted to the point where I began to serve only myself. This passage speaks directly to us in law enforcement. We are called to be servants.

I have learned that if the Bible mentions anything, it is important. If it mentions it twice, I better pay particular attention to it. In this passage Jesus tells us three times (verse four, six, and eighteen), "Then your Father, who sees what is done in secret, will reward you." We all want to be recognized for a job well done. Instead of winning a cheap earthly reward, why not save up for a heavenly one?

Highlights from this Read: We can't help but notice the Lord's Prayer in this passage. Verse nine through fifteen is probably the most recognized prayer of all time. I think it is interesting that we know this prayer because in most churches the entire congregation recites it. Jesus teaches us this prayer as one to be prayed in secret. We use it as a public group prayer.

Verses sixteen through eighteen give us some direction on fasting. The church I grew up in did not practice this so fasting was very "out of the box" for me. It is an opportunity for a deep spiritual connection with the Father.

I find verse fourteen particularly alarming. If I choose not to forgive someone who crosses me then God will not forgive me for all the times I have sinned, which is constant. I not only have to ask Him for forgiveness but I have to get into the attitude of forgiving others.

Investigation (Resources): Luke 11:2-4

Officer Safety (Principles for the LEO to live by): Attitude is key.

Matthew 6:19-21

Briefing: What kind of retirement do you have? Do you put back money into a savings account? Does your department provide a retirement system? I have paid into my police retirement for over twenty years now. There will come a time in my life where it will pay off and I can sit back and enjoy the rest of my life.

Dispatch/Assignment:
Read Matthew 6:19-21 and 25:31-46.

On the Street: Are you the kind of person who saves up for a vacation or someone who spends the money as it comes in and enjoys life?

Jesus tells us to live life in a way that we work towards the goal of heaven. Paul gives the analogy of a runner who trains hard, not to be in shape but to win the race. His goal is not to compete, it's to win. It is an attitude and a focus not just an extracurricular activity.

This kind of living takes a total "buy in" commitment. It is like the kind of commitment a LEO makes when the moment of truth is staring him in the face. You arrive on the scene of an active shooter. You don't have time to wait for SWAT you have to stop the threat! Take a deep breath, be sharp mentally, focus and dive in! As a Christian this is how I envision my journey with Christ. I want to be "all in". No matter how bad it gets, I have to have the courage to move forward.

If we live this out, as Christians, we will be storing up for ourselves treasures in heaven. The things of this earth will burn. All of it will be gone, your favorite gun, your house and your boat. All of the things you have worked all your life for will be gone. All, except the things you did to benefit the kingdom of God.

Highlights from this Read: Where is your treasure? Another good way of asking this question is what do you look forward to? What do you spend your money on? When you have free time, what do you spend that time doing? This is where your treasure is.

This is a question of flesh versus spirit. It is a very common underlying theme throughout the Bible. An understanding of your flesh versus your spirit comes more into play the further your journey with Christ goes. It is essential to your Christian walk.

Investigation (Resources): For other verses on how to live this life of storing up treasures in heaven see Matthew 6:1-4, 7:15-27. 1 Corinthians 9:24-27 Paul talks about running the race. A companion story is found in Luke 11:34-36.

Officer Safety (Principles for the LEO to live by): Christ desires to be the treasure of your heart. Pray to God and ask Him to reveal to you how this should look in your life, then act on it.

Matthew 6:22-24

Briefing: Do you have "cop eyes"? Do you look at situations at work differently than you do when you are off duty? Usually you have the ability to see criminal activity no matter if you or on or off duty?

Dispatch/Assignment:
Read Matthew 6:22-24. At the conclusion of this lesson, check your sight.

On the Street: We addressed the question of "cop eyes" in the briefing. Now I want to ask if you have "spiritual sight". Are you able to see God at work all around you? Are you able to see a situation and know that God is in control?

What do you think Jesus was talking about here when He was asking about good eyes versus bad eyes? Where do your eyes gravitate? In my experience, they tend to look at where my heart says to look. In other words, what my heart desires is usually what my eyes look at. If I desire a new gun and there are two magazines in front of me, one is a boat magazine and the other is a gun magazine, which do you think I will pick up? If your eyes are constantly looking at objects that you covet or lust after, can you guess what your heart is wanting?

As a teen, my favorite rock group was Petra. One of my favorite songs of theirs was "Computer Brains", written by Bob Hartman. The song is based on 2 Corinthians 10:5 which says, "We demolish arguments and every pretension that sets itself up against the knowledge of God, and we take captive every thought to make it obedient to Christ".

The chorus says, "Computer brains, put garbage in. Computer brains, get garbage out".

The question we have to ask ourselves is, "what kind of stuff are you allowing into your heart?" Would God be pleased by the images you look at?

Just as we have a "duty to act" as a law enforcement officer, we also have a "duty to act" as a Christian. We have to take a stand and not allow the filth of this world to enter into our hearts. We have been trained on how to take someone captive. We need to learn how to train our mind to take our thoughts captive.

Investigation (Resources): Romans 7:7-8:39, 1 Peter 1:13, Philippians 4:8-9, 2 Corinthians 10:5, Matthew 15:11-20

Officer Safety (Principles for the LEO to live by): Our spirit is at war with our flesh. We will choose to serve one or the other. Which one will you serve?

Matthew 6:25-34

Briefing: Police have the highest suicide rate in the nation. They have the second highest divorce rate and are twice as likely as a non LEO to become an alcoholic.

Dispatch/Assignment:
Sit down with your co-workers and put together a list of how each of you deal with stress then share your list with each other. Read Matthew 6:25-34.

On the Street: Hans Selye is the foremost researcher on stress in the world. He says that police work is "the most stressful occupation in America, even surpassing the formidable stresses of air traffic control." I know this does not come as a shock to anyone who does this job, but knowing it, and seeing someone else recognize it are two different things.

We can't change the kind of stress that we deal with but we can work on the way we deal with it. Jesus gives us a simple way of dealing with worry and stress. He lays out all of our basic needs and tells us that it is silly for us to kill ourselves by worrying about things that are totally out of our control. It is pointless.

Jesus gives us the key in verse thirty-three. He says, "But seek first His kingdom". We have to take our focus off of ourselves and our problems and seek Him first. "And His righteousness" says to me that we should pattern our lives after His life in an attempt to live righteous. Jesus finishes out the verse by saying, "and all these things will be given to you as well."

There is life in verse thirty-four (as in most of the Bible) where Jesus commands us, "Therefore do not worry about tomorrow, for tomorrow will worry about itself. Each day has enough trouble of its own." If I could just remember this verse I could greatly reduce the amount of stress I have in my life.

<u>Highlights from this Read:</u> In verse twenty-nine Jesus referred to Solomon. Solomon was an Israelite king who was granted wisdom from God, so much so that there had never been a man up to that point who could surpass his wisdom.

<u>Investigation (Resources):</u> After my grandmother died, I was blessed with the opportunity to look through her Bible and see the notes that she had written on the pages. In the margin by 1 Peter 5:6-7 she wrote, "This is the solution to depression". Read it and see what you think.

Another great resource on living a life with less stress is the book of Proverbs. To see this passage from Luke's perspective see Luke 12:22-31.

<u>Officer Safety (Principles for the LEO to live by):</u> I challenge you to get into a daily read and prayer life with the Lord. I believe if you do this and allow God to work in your life you will see a dramatic reduction of stress in your life. When you feel stressed or depressed seek fellowship with another believer.

Matthew 7:1-6

Briefing: Can you think of a job that requires someone to judge people more than being a LEO? My first thought was yes, a judge, but in the majority of cases that I have been involved with it is not a judge who actually decides the outcome of a case but the jury.

Dispatch/Assignment:
Webster's dictionary defines judge as, "to form an opinion about through careful weighing of evidence." Read Matthew 7:1-6.

On the Street: If I read these couple of verses I could easily get the wrong impression of judging people. How I define judging could affect my opinion of what I do as an LEO. If God's word told me not to judge people's motives, their truthfulness or intentions I could not be an LEO.

So what does the Bible say about judging? Leviticus 19:15 says, "Do not pervert justice; do not show partiality to the poor or favoritism to the great, but judge your neighbor fairly". There is a great passage in Proverbs that reads like a speech at a rookie academy graduation. It says, "speak up for those who cannot speak for themselves, for the rights of all who are destitute. Speak up and judge fairly, defend the rights of the poor and needy."

I believe that He is telling us to take into account what really matters while making judgments, our heart and our attitude. We tend to judge hypocritically and with a self righteous attitude.

This is a question many new Christian LEOs struggle with. God's word is full of examples where we are told to judge fairly. As an LEO, we are truth seekers. Most calls for police involve a law enforcement officer to make a decision based on facts and give objective, fair judgments. This lines up with scripture.

In verse six Jesus tells us to have discretion and use discernment. If Jesus was telling us not to judge in verse one then He would not be giving us advice about judging others in verse six. In John 7:24 Jesus said, "stop judging by mere appearances, and make a right judgment."

Highlights from this Read: Verse three paints a funny word picture of a person with a plank of wood in his eye. Jesus wants us to help each other, but we have to exercise humble judgment with the right attitude and motives. It should be out of love.

In verse six Jesus specifically uses dogs and pigs in His description. In His day dogs were mostly wild animals and pigs were unclean. He is describing a particular type of person.

Investigation (Resources): For more scripture on judging read; Deuteronomy 1:16, 2 Chronicles 19:7, Proverbs 24:23-25, and Romans chapter thirteen. Also see Luke 6:41-42.

Officer Safety (Principles for the LEO to live by): Be the impartial judge that God has called you to be. 2 Chronicles 19:7, "Now let the fear of the Lord be upon you, judge carefully, for with the Lord your God there is no injustice or partiality or bribery." When making judgments, be God's ambassador and make the decisions based on God's standards.

Matthew 7:7-12

Briefing: Do you pray on duty? Do you pray for your department or agency? Do you ever pray for that one officer who seems so lost that not even Billy Graham could lead him to Christ? What things in your job could you pray for that are seemingly impossible for God to work through?

Dispatch/Assignment:
Think of a time when you prayed for someone in your department. Read Matthew 7:7-12.

On the Street: In this section we see Jesus teaching us to pray. Jesus says, "Ask, seek and knock." If you never ask, why would you expect to receive? If you never knock, why would you expect for someone to open the door? If you never seek, why would you expect to find? Christians cannot have an entitlement attitude.

I often hear people say, "God helps those who help themselves" but I can't find this in scripture. God wants us to ask Him. He wants conversation and communication. I can do all things through Christ who strengthens me but apart from God I can do nothing.

How does this apply to the LEO? The questions in the briefing above are a clue. I challenge you to pray for that one person in your work place that you think will never come to know Christ. Don't just pray once and give up, but pray daily or better yet, every time they cross your path (James 5:16).

Not only does God want us to pray and communicate with Him, He wants to give us good things. I love how Jesus compares us to children asking their father for a gift. This is exactly what it is! As a father I can relate to having the desire to give my kids good gifts.

Jesus sums this section up by giving, what we now call, the Golden Rule, "do to others what you would have them do to you". This is contrary to the "rule" my first training officer gave me. It went something like this, "Treat people how they expect to be treated". Most people I came into contact with had been poorly treated for most of their lives. That's usually why LEO's are inserted into a situation. For us to treat them like what they had become accustomed to did not live up to the Golden Rule standard. Proverbs 11:27 says, "He who seeks good finds goodwill but evil comes to him who searches for it."

Highlights from this Read: In verse twelve Jesus said, "for this sums up the Law and the Prophets". This is interesting because He also alluded to this in Matthew 22:40 when He was answering the question of which is the greatest commandment.

Investigation (Resources): Philippians 4:13 I can do all things, John 15:1-8 apart from God I can do nothing, Romans 8:28 all thing work for the good of those who love Him. Jeremiah 29:11. All good things come from God, James 1:17, the effectual prayer of a righteous man, James 5:16, Luke 18:1-8 the woman who wore down the judge. Also see Luke 11:9-13.

Officer Safety (Principles for the LEO to live by): I don't believe that in our human flesh, we will ever be able to comprehend the power of prayer. We desperately need to be in prayer for our fellow officers, supervisors, and administrations.

Matthew 7:13-14

Briefing: Not everybody is cut out to be a Law Enforcement Officer. Police Officers don't follow the crowd. When shots are fired and people are running away from the danger, cops are running towards it. We talk different, we act different, we think different... We Are Different.

Dispatch/Assignment:
How are you different? Read Matthew 7:13-14.

On the Street: There is a sign in our workout room that reads, "If it were easy, this room would be full".

Growing up my dad used to tell me, "Son, if something sounds too good to be true, then it probably is". We all know this to be the case, yet time and time again, we see people falling for the easy way out, the get rich scam and the short cut. I could go on and on. You practice like you play but first you have to practice. Hard work pays off in the end. Do the work up front and enjoy the benefits later.

Christ does not call us to what is easy but what is worthy. Most LEO's have some kind of retirement, a reward for years of hard work. I look at my life here on Earth the same way. I need to put in the hard work for Christ now so that when I am finished (death) I will have a retirement (heaven). Maybe that's why Ephesians 6:7-8, "Serve wholeheartedly, as if you were serving the Lord, not men, because you know that the Lord will reward everyone for whatever good he does, whether he is slave or free."

We have to go against the grain, we have to live our lives in such a way that people know we are different than the world. We live for someone greater than ourselves. Growing up I was blessed to listen to Pastor Ron Horton preach messages that I have fallen back on all my life. I remember him asking this question during a sermon, "Have you run into Satan today? If not you may be going in the same direction."

The brave men and women I work with have no problem rushing into places where everyone is fleeing. I want that same courage and bravery demonstrated in my Christian life. I want to be courageous for Jesus.

Highlights from this Read: Jesus is the gate (John 10:7-10) and the shepherd. We know His voice and follow Him.

Investigation (Resources): In 1 Corinthians 16 Paul instructs the Corinthians about serving. Mark 8:34-35 and Matthew 10:38 are passages that Jesus tells us to take up our cross and follow Him. John 10:7-10 explains Jesus is the gate.

Officer Safety (Principles for the LEO to live by): We have to make a conscious decision to live contrary to this world, to live for Jesus Christ. We have to live in such a way that we meet Satan head on.

Matthew 7:15-23

Briefing: When you are off duty do you carry a gun under your shirt or in your purse? When you go out to eat, do you always sit facing the door? Do you scope out the nearest exit? Do you size up the person next to you in line at the grocery store? Do people know you are a LEO?

Dispatch/Assignment:
Take a moment to think about what others perception of you might be. Read Matthew 7:15-23.

On the Street: When I was in the police academy there were cadets who would hang a police shirt in their back windshield. They wanted the whole world to know they were the police. The truth is they were not. They did not have a gun, a badge, or a commission. These guys wanted everyone to think they were cops. They were proud of the profession they were getting into.

I have a good friend who is a fellow Officer, serving in the same department and on the same shift. He is a Police Officer on duty and off duty. When he is off duty he wears police association t-shirts, his tactical boots and police ball cap. If you engage him in conversation you can tell he's a cop by the words he uses. Sometimes he will even slip in a 10-4 instead of saying yes. He can walk in a crowded grocery store and within minutes everyone either recognizes he is a police officer or they think he is casing the place.

Do you approach your life as a Christian the same way? Are you excited to be known as a Christian? Do you live your life in such a way that people see that you are making an effort to be like Christ.

Has anyone ever told you, "Do as I say, not as I do". This is a frightening place to be. Jesus said, "by their fruit you will recognize them". It is the same principle when someone tells you that so-and-so goes to their church. Your reaction is shock and you say something like, WOW!! I didn't know they were a Christian! (Going to church does not make you a Christian). What scares me even more is thinking how many people have said that about me? Do you live your life in such a way that there is no mistaking who you are? Do people know you are a Christian?

<u>Highlights from this Read:</u> In verse twenty-one Jesus says, "Not everyone who says to me Lord, Lord, will enter the kingdom of heaven, but only the one who does the will of my Father who is in heaven." In Luke 6:46 Jesus asks the question, "Why do you call me Lord, Lord, and do not do what I say?" If we are truly Christians and call Jesus our Lord, we have to produce fruit, it has to be visible for others to see, we have to live like He has called us to live.

<u>Investigation (Resources):</u> You can find the listing of Fruits of the Spirit in Galatians 5:22.

<u>Officer Safety (Principles for the LEO to live by):</u> We have to make a conscious decision to live contrary to this world, to live for Jesus Christ.

Matthew 7:24-29

Briefing: I would be willing to bet that ninety percent of your basic police skills were learned in academy. You will build on that foundation all of your career.

What are your foundational beliefs in law enforcement and in your Christian life? Read Matthew 7:24-29.

On the Street: If I asked you what the foundational law enforcement training was you would probably list things like arrest skills, shooting, basic law and policies. These are the skills and basic training that will last you your entire career.

When I was in high school, my dad quit teaching school to build houses. While working for him I learned some things about foundations. There are a couple of principles about foundation work. If the foundation is not done properly, a builder won't waste their time building a house on it. Your foundational training, police academy, is so important that if you don't graduate, you don't get certified or ultimately hired.

Another principle about foundations is that once you start it you don't start anything else until it's finished. You can't start working on the roof or putting in windows until the foundation is complete and ready. Have you ever known a police officer who was sent back to academy to re-learn the basics? I haven't. Luckily this is not the case with Christ. As long as you're breathing you have a chance.

Foundation building is serious work. Your foundation in Christ is extremely important. So much so that the amount of importance you place on it determines the kind of ground you build on. If you prioritize it as a matter of life and death with eternal consequences and that resolve in your life is the compass that points you in the direction you should go, it's a safe bet that you have built your house on solid ground.

If you listened to the Word and thought it was good in theory but not something you really want to live your life by, or you just don't have time for, this lesson is for you. If you think that just because you walked the isle and prayed a prayer when you were little that you are ok, you might find yourself on sinking sand.

It's not too late. Repent basically means to make a one hundred and eighty degree turn around from where you are. If you find yourself standing on a sinking slab that was put down years ago with no walls or roof, you can make a new start.

Highlights from this Read: Both builders heard the words of Jesus; however, only the first one put them into practice.

Investigation (Resources): For information on how to re-start, look in the back of this study guide for "How do I become a Christian?" Also see Luke 6:47-49.

Officer Safety (Principles for the LEO to live by): If you are reading this devotional I pray that you have a firm foundation. These studies are like the blueprints for building your workshop. For plans on building the house that is talked about in these verses, read the Master's blueprint, The Holy Bible.

Matthew 8:1-4

Briefing: Have you ever had an issue with someone in authority over you? Did you rebel against that authority? I'm pretty sure we all have had this experience.

Dispatch/Assignment:
Who has authority over you?
Read Matthew 8:1-4.

On the Street: As law enforcement officers we are given a certain amount of authority. Our authority might come from our governing bodies but Romans 7 tells us that it ultimately comes from God.

Jesus is God. He did not have to submit to anyone. We see in Philippians 2:5-11 that Jesus humbled Himself and died on the cross in an act of obedience to the Father.

When Jesus was being tried by Pilot He submitted to the authority but clarified for Pilot and us that it was God who put Pilot in power. Pilot had no power except that power that God had given him as the Roman Governor of Jerusalem.

In this passage we see another example of Jesus respecting the earthly authority that God had put in place. Even though Jesus was not under the authority of the priest, He did not want to be a stumbling block to others. Jesus goes out of His way to respect the priestly authority of the Jews. In order to lead by example He tells the man with leprosy to go and show himself to the priest and offer the gift that Moses commanded. Jesus told him to do this as "testimony to them". This was not a testimony to Himself or God but to the priest, the earthly authority that God had set up.

Highlights from this Read: Jesus often went to the mountains for quiet time with His Father as we see in Matthew 5:1, 14:23, 15:29 and 17:1. At the start of this passage He was coming down from teaching the Sermon on the Mount. These crowds followed Him throughout His ministry but did they know He intended them to follow Him to the cross? In Matthew 10:38 Jesus said, "anyone who does not take his cross and follow me is not worthy of me."

Jesus healed a man with leprosy. This was a man, that by Jewish law (Leviticus 13:45-46), was not to be touched and anyone who touched him would be considered unclean. Jesus could have healed this guy with His words alone but Jesus reached out His hand and touched him. This is a person who people have avoided touching ever since he got the disease. Jesus knew the power of the touch and had great compassion and love for this man.

Investigation (Resources): Romans 13:1-7 on authority. John 19:10-11 Jesus speaks of Pilot's authority. Luke 5:24 is about Jesus' authority. Leviticus 14:2-32 is the law concerning the gift to be given to the priest. For more reading on this passage, see Mark 1:40-44 and Luke 5:12-14.

Officer Safety (Principles for the LEO to live by): Make sure you stay obedient to God and obey the authorities that are in your life, remember who placed them there.

Matthew 8:5-13

Briefing: If Jesus were living today, as He was in New Testament times, what would be your jurisdiction's protocol concerning Him? You know He draws a crowd. Some people love Him and some people want to kill Him. As an officer dispatched to one or more of these gatherings you may have the opportunity to listen to Him and even see Him perform miracles.

Dispatch/Assignment:
What are some of the characteristics you look for in a leader? Read Matthew 8:5-13.

On the Street: Jesus made Capernaum His home town and the center of His activities. This is the town He returned to for rest after long journeys.

During Jesus' entire life, all of Israel was occupied by Rome. There were Roman soldiers in every major town. Capernaum was one of the cities that had a permanent Roman army presence. Roman soldiers were the peace keepers of the time, the police force.

The Romans that were stationed in Capernaum would have been very familiar with Jesus. When He returned home from a journey crowds would gather. Because of this, Roman soldiers would be called out in force to make sure there were no riots. This might explain why the Roman Centurion in these verses knew who Jesus was. He would have been there when Jesus taught and performed miracles.

A Centurion was a Roman soldier in charge of one hundred soldiers. He was their supervisor, leader, sergeant. This particular Centurion is spoken of in Matthew and also Luke. There are a total of eighteen verses describing his encounter with Jesus. It amazes me that we see so much of his character in just a few verses.

This Centurion was a great leader. We know this because his men followed him without question. This is easy to see because of his statement to Jesus, "I tell one to do this and he does it". Because of his soldier's obedience to his authority, he is able to understand what absolute authority is. He had no doubts that if Jesus said for it to be done, it absolutely would be done exactly as He said. His soldiers' obedience is a testament to him.

This Centurion was humble. He was not arrogant. A good example of an arrogant military leader is found in 2 Kings 5:1-15.

He took time to get to know the people around him and he invested in people's lives. This is seen in his knowing and believing in Jesus so completely.

This guy was compassionate. You can see it in his statement to Jesus, "my servant lies at home paralyzed and in terrible suffering". This was not just some servant, whom he could replace, this servant was important to him.

The Bible does not say this but I believe that this Centurion was declared righteous even though the Holy Spirit had not yet come. The reason I believe this is because, like Abraham in Genesis 15:6, he demonstrated a faith that was absolute.

He was a generous man. In the version in Luke we see that he built the Jewish synagogue in Capernaum. This is found in Luke 7:5. His faith was contagious. We see, again in Luke, where the Jewish elders of Capernaum believed in Jesus' deity. This is not something we see a lot of in the gospels. Usually, the Chief priest and the elders were against Jesus but here they go to Jesus and ask Him to heal the Centurion's servant.

He had respect for the Jewish people and their customs. In Acts 10:23-48 we read about Peter's encounter with another Centurion named Cornelius. Peter tells Cornelius that it was against Jewish law for him to associate with or visit a Gentile. This is probably the reason that our Centurion tells Jesus that he is undeserving of having Jesus come to his house.

This Centurion lived out the command given to us in Luke 10:27 "Love the Lord your God with all your heart and with all your soul and with all your strength and with all your mind and, Love your neighbor as yourself."

This Centurion had childlike faith. The Bible tells us that we should all have this kind of faith, Matthew 11:25 and 18:3.

Highlights from this Read: In verse eight, when the Centurion says, "I do not deserve to have you come under my roof" this is also the attitude that John the Baptist had when it came to being in the presence of Christ. John said that he was not even worthy to untie Jesus' sandals.

In verse ten, the Bible only mentions Jesus being amazed twice. The first is here because of the faith of the Centurion and the other is in Mark 6:6 because of the unbelief of the people in Nazareth.

Investigation (Resources): Matthew 4:13-17 on Capernaum. Luke 7:1-10 is Luke's perspective of the story.

Officer Safety (Principles for the LEO to live by): We all need to strive to have a character that points to Christ and to live by Luke 10:27.

Matthew 8:14-17

Briefing: When you get a radio call, dispatch, or assignment do you respond in a timely manner or do you put it on your list of things to do?

Dispatch/Assignment:
Are you busy with kingdom work? Read Matthew 8:14-17.

On the Street: When Jesus cures Peter's mother-in-law of fever, the Bible says, "She got up and began to wait on Him". The very next sentence Jesus is "driving out spirits with a word". These two passages put together fit like a hand in a glove with Matthew 12:43-45.

"When an impure spirit comes out of a person, it goes through arid places seeking rest and does not find it. Then it says, 'I will return to the house I left.' When it arrives, it finds the house unoccupied, swept clean and put in order. Then it goes and takes with it seven other spirits more wicked than itself, and they go in and live there. And the final condition of that person is worse than the first. That is how it will be with this wicked generation."

When reading this I get a sense of urgency. Time is of the essence. Have you ever heard someone say, "God's timing is perfect"? When God opens a door for you, go through it, don't hesitate. When God told Abram to go to a new country that he had never been before (Genesis 12:1-4) he got up and went.

If Christ has done a work in your life, saved you from Hell and forgiven your sins, then it is time to get to work. The house is swept clean. What are you going to do?

Highlights from this Read: Peter was married. We don't know anything about his wife but we know he had a mother-in-law.

It is very important to check your motives when doing your work for the Lord. Works don't get you into heaven and works with the wrong attitude do you no good either. Luke 10:38-42 is a beautiful story about Mary and her sister Martha. Martha was busy getting lunch ready and serving everyone but she was upset with Mary because she was sitting around listening to Jesus and not helping with the work. Martha gets so upset that she goes to Jesus and tells Him to tell Mary to help her. Jesus tells her, "you are worried and upset about many things, but only one thing is needed. Mary has chosen what is better, and it will not be taken away from her." We have to be serving with an attitude of love.

Investigation (Resources): Isaiah 53:4 is the prophecy that was fulfilled. For other accounts of this story see Mark 1:29-34 and Luke 4:38-41

Officer Safety (Principles for the LEO to live by): We have to get to work on kingdom matters. If you have not gotten an assignment from God, pray that He will show you what He has for you. Remember, He will not give you more than you can handle.

Matthew 8:18-22

Briefing: There is an officer in the agency where I work who had prior police experience in another police agency. He has been with our agency for over ten years but is always saying how things were so much better at the last place he worked. He can't move forward because he spends all of his time looking backwards.

Dispatch/Assignment:
Are you prepared and committed? You have to be both to fully follow Christ. Read Matthew 8:18-22 and Luke 9:57-62.

On the Street: Crowds followed Jesus wherever He went. He was a very popular figure. It seems that everyone wanted a piece of Him.

Jesus did not always seem to enjoy being the center of attention. We see in other passages that Jesus would often find quiet places to go pray. As I read the first verse of this passage, I couldn't help but think that He needed some prayer time at this moment. The crowd persisted. They wanted to go where He was going. They were coming up to Him and pledge their willingness to follow Him.

Jesus told the first man, a teacher of the law, this is not some lavish tour they are going on. Jesus is trusting God to provide for their entire journey. They are not calling ahead and getting reservations to the top inn in town. If you want to see how Jesus travels, jump forward to Matthew 10:5-20. Jesus was asking the prospective followers if they were prepared.

The same account is found in Luke 9:57-60, but Luke goes further. In this account we see Jesus also asking if they are committed. In 9:62 Jesus said, "No one who puts his hand to the plow and looks back is fit for service in the kingdom of God". Try this sometime at home with a rake in the sand or dirt. Walk in a straight path pushing your rake, then look back. When you return to looking forward you will see that your straight path has gone off course. Are you willing to go the distance? If you are you will have to leave your junk behind.

Highlights from this Read: In verse nineteen, the teacher of the law was too eager and did not consider the cost. In verse twenty-one we see the disciple who asks to first go bury his father is reminiscent of Luke 14:15-24. This is where people are invited to the banquet but when the time comes for the feast they all come up with excuses as to why they could not come.

Investigation (Resources): Luke 9:57-60 and 14:25-27.

Officer Safety (Principles for the LEO to live by): Are you prepared and are you committed?

Matthew 8:23-27

Briefing: As a LEO it is our job to be in control. We get called to situations where control has been lost and our job is to restore it. We have to maintain control of ourselves and the situations around us. That is just part of our job. I believe that if we let it, this can bleed over into every aspect of our lives. We have to guard against being control freaks.

Dispatch/Assignment:
Who is in control? Read Matthew 8:23-27.

On the Street: Jesus is in a boat with some of the most experienced sailors in the area. Andrew, Peter, James and John have been fishing this lake all of their lives. These men were in control of this vessel.

What sin do you have in your life that you have total control over? You don't need help because you have the experience and know how to handle it. "You control it, it does not control you", have you ever caught yourself saying this? How about this one, "I can stop myself any time I want".

This must have been the worst storm the disciples had ever seen. These experienced fishermen and sailors could not handle what was happening. This was a storm they could not control.

Have you ever been in a storm/situation that you could not control? Maybe it was a bad call at work, or maybe a family fight? We have all been in situation that no matter how hard we tried we could not establish or regain control. In fact, the harder we tried, the worse it got.

I would be willing to bet that the disciples tried everything they could to maintain control of their boat. It was only when all else failed that they cried out to Jesus. Do you think there was a point early on in the troubled storm that they could have called to Jesus to "fix" it, but they just didn't want to bother Him? Was He teaching them a lesson? I think so. I need to relinquish control, ultimately it's a pride issue, and ask Jesus to step in before it's too late.

Highlights from this Read: This passage follows the lesson on being prepared and committed. Giving up control seems to be the next natural step in becoming a Christ follower.

Do you think the Centurion, that we read about earlier, would have been amazed at Jesus being able to calm the storm? Don't be afraid of Jesus using you for His service. He left the Centurion right where he was. Jesus' calling does not mean you have to go to China. He can use you right where you are, in your agency. Be a law enforcement officer for Christ.

Investigation (Resources): Mark 4:36-41, Luke 8:22-25 and Matthew 14:22-33

Officer Safety (Principles for the LEO to live by): Be committed, be prepared and be willing to give up control of your life to Christ for what is He calling you?

Matthew 8:28-34

Briefing: Imagine if someone came up to you with the winning lottery ticket and tried to give it to you. You know that this jackpot is worth millions. You throw your hands up and say, "No thanks, I don't play the lottery".

Dispatch/Assignment:
Missed opportunities. Read Matthew 8:28-34.

On the Street: Have you ever missed an opportunity and later regretted it? I don't think that in all of history there has ever been a greater missed opportunity than the one told in these verses.

When I was eighteen I went to FCA (Fellowship of Christian Athletes) summer camp in Estes Park, Colorado. There was a young man in our group that had never received Christ as his Lord and Savior. At the end of the week I was talking to him about coming to faith in Jesus and our need for Him in our lives. I was so excited about getting to share with him and be a part of a decision that would impact eternity.

I'll never forget what he told me at the end of the night. He wanted to put off any decision to get involved in a relationship with Jesus until he had the opportunity to party and have fun. I can remember the feeling of shock and confusion that came over me. I didn't understand it.

One thing I will say, at least he was honest with himself and didn't make a decision based on guilt. If he had, and it was not a true repentance and confession, he might have gone all his life under the impression that he had given his life to Christ and was saved.

Highlights from this Read: In verse thirty, the people of Gadarenes were Gentiles. We know this because, to the Jews, pigs were unclean animals. This is a highlight for me because we find out later that Jesus has come to save us all, not just the Jewish people.

Whenever I read verse thirty-two I always end up with the same question. When Jesus allowed the demons to enter the pigs, the pigs ran into the lake and died. What happened to the demons after that?

Investigation (Resources): Mark 5:1-17 and Luke 8:26-37.

Officer Safety (Principles for the LEO to live by): Have you missed an opportunity to accept Christ? If so, it is not too late.

Matthew 9:1-8

Briefing: One of the saddest days I have experienced in my career was the death of a fellow officer and good friend. It happened early in my career at a time when I was not praying for my brothers and sisters in blue. I was not even sure of his walk with Christ. I regret that.

Dispatch/Assignment: Do you pray for your fellow Law enforcement officers? Do you think it makes a difference?

On the Street: What is prayer and why is it so important? Simply put, prayer is communication with God. If you have ever been in a relationship you know that one of the most important elements of keeping it healthy and alive is communication. If I went a month without talking to my wife, our relationship would start to deteriorate.

The same can be said with our relationship with God. We are His children and He wants a relationship with us. If my relationship with God is not good, chances are it's because I don't communicate with Him. Jesus tells us that we have not because we ask not (James 4:2). Matthew 7:7 says, "Ask and it will be given to you".

The Bible tells us to pray for our fellow officers. 1 Timothy 2:1-2 says, "I urge, then, first of all, that requests, prayers, intercession and thanksgiving be made for everyone, for kings and *all those in authority*, that we may live peaceful and quiet lives in all godliness and holiness". I believe that God hears our prayers and protects us.

Jesus tells us this when He taught His disciples how to pray. We call it the Lord's Prayer.

Here are some of the things we should be praying. We need to pray for the Officers who work with us to come to a saving knowledge of Christ. We need to pray for each other's families, relationships, finances and safety. We need to pray for the ability to do the right thing, to act with integrity and be a Christ like example to others. We also need to pray for our Chief's and their staff to make decisions based on Truth and lead by example. This is a short list.

I always get a renewed conviction to pray for others when I read these verses. The thing that strikes me is that the paralytic does not appear to say anything. Jesus saw the faith of his friends as they brought him to Christ. That was enough for Jesus to heal him. I like to think that He will do the same for us as we pray for our fellow officers and their families.

Highlights from this Read: In verse one, it says Jesus returned to His own town, Capernaum.

In verse two, Jesus heals the paralytic of his spiritual illness before healing him of his physical condition.

In verse six, Jesus heals the man of his paralysis to prove to the crowd that He is the Christ.

Investigation (Resources): You can find more about prayer in James 4. For passages about the good gifts read Luke 11. James 5:16. Mark 2:3-12 and Luke 5:18-26 are companion passages from their perspective.

Officer Safety (Principles for the LEO to live by): Start talking to God and just pour out your heart. It does make a difference.

Matthew 9:9-13

Briefing: What is your definition of mercy? How do you apply it in your job?

Dispatch/Assignment: Research your laws and policies and see how many times you come across an option to offer mercy to an offender.

On the Street: Webster's dictionary has two good definitions of mercy. The first one defines it as compassion to an offender or to one subject to one's power. The second one is a blessing that is an act of divine favor or compassion.

How does this apply to my job? Certain areas of our law enforcement duties give us discretion when taking enforcement action. When I was a younger officer, I took that to mean that I should arrest everyone I caught violating the law. As I have aged, I realize that it means the opposite of that. The law allowed for me to take enforcement action on everyone that I observed violating the law, discretion (mercy) gave me the legal authority to have mercy in certain situations.

I believe that God has called men and women to this job for the expressed purpose of carrying out justice. Romans 13:1-5 says that God has put people in positions of authority. He chose who He wanted to be there. These people are God's servants to do good. It goes further to state, "but if you do wrong, be afraid, for he does not bear the sword for nothing." These in authority (police) are to be God's agents, to do good or bring punishment.

Jesus desires mercy, not sacrifice. An act of mercy and an act of sacrifice can look identical. The difference is intention and attitude. Jesus is warning us of our heart condition. Mercy requires personal involvement (an act of the heart), while sacrifice is most often impersonal (an act of the will).

Highlights from this Read: Verse nine tells about Matthew. In other versions we see Matthew is called Levi. This can be a really fun independent study. See how many times, in the Bible, God changes someone's name.

Matthew was a tax collector. Tax collectors were the most hated people in all of Israel. I wonder how accepted he was by the other disciples.

In verse eleven, the Pharisees were at Matthew's house watching Jesus eating with tax collectors. What were they doing there?

Investigation (Resources): Mark 2:14–17 and Luke 5:27–32.

Officer Safety (Principles for the LEO to live by): How often do you show mercy or give mercy? Is your attitude towards mercy the same when you are off duty as it is when you are on duty?

Matthew 9:14-17

Briefing: Actions must mirror the situation. You would not pull your weapon and perform a felony traffic stop on a little old lady for not wearing her seatbelt. If it was winter in Chicago, you would not show up for a patrol shift wearing a bathing suit.

Do you have people in your agency whose favorite phrase is, "That's the way we've always done it".

On the Street: It would be totally inappropriate for Jesus' disciples to fast while He was in their presence. The act of fasting does not fit the situation.

Just because that was what everyone else did or that's the way we've always done it, does not make it right.

Wedding parties don't last forever. They are brief periods of time to enjoy friendships before a major life change occurs. Jesus knew He was only going to be here for a short period of time and while He was here, His disciples needed to focus on learning all they could from Him, not just performing religious practices. He was more interested in spending quality time with them, not just watching to see if they practiced the correct religious laws.

Jesus was bringing understanding to the way things were supposed to be. He was teaching that murder was not just the act of killing someone, but hating your brother, as well. Adultery could happen in your heart and mind easier than the physical act, but was just as dangerous and corrupt. These were not new teachings. This was how He intended it to be understood from the beginning.

Jesus' message needed a new vessel to carry it. This would be the calling of the Church. Israel had become too rigid and unresponsive and would not be the catalyst to carry His message to the world. Judaism's emphasis on legalism and rituals was incompatible with Jesus' gospel.

In this day and age we are not very familiar with wine skins or sewing patches on clothing. What is Jesus trying to teach us? This is the explanation of why His disciples are not fasting. Fasting, like pouring new wine into old wineskins, was an act that did not fit the situation. Old vessels trying to carry new messages were only new to the people of the time, not to God.

Highlights from this Read: John's disciples come to Jesus with this question of fasting. I can't help but wonder if they stopped to compare notes with Andrew, Peter's brother. Andrew started off as John the Baptist's disciple and would have known the ones who came asking.

Investigation (Resources): Mark 2:18-22 and Luke 5:33-39

Officer Safety (Principles for the LEO to live by): Jesus is not looking for us to do what we've always done. We have to be the vessel for His Word. This means living different from the world, living for Him.

Matthew 9:18-34

Briefing: In our line of work we meet hundreds, if not thousands of people. Unfortunately our introduction into their life is due to a crisis. They are often desperate for a solution or we (LEO) would not be involved.

Dispatch/Assignment:
How desperate are you for Christ? Read Matthew 9:18-34.

On the Street: In this series of accounts, Jesus is coming into contact with people who are in crisis. These individuals are expecting Jesus to do the impossible. They are desperate for a miracle.

The first crisis involves a leader from the local synagogue. His daughter has just died. I have a daughter who is not much older than his daughter. I can't imagine how desperate I would have been in this situation.

While on His way to the synagogue leader's home Jesus is approached by a woman who has been ill for twelve years. Her life has been ruined by her condition. Not only did she suffer physical pain but mental and emotional pain. According to Jewish law (Leviticus 15:25) she was unclean for the entire twelve years which meant that she could not socialize with anyone or go to worship at the synagogue because of her uncleanliness. She would have been a social outcast.

According to Jewish law, both of these encounters would have made Jesus "unclean". The religious leaders were more concerned with keeping the letter of the law than the compassion they should have had for each other. This is called legalism. Jesus spoke of this in verse thirteen when He says, "I desire mercy, not sacrifice". Jesus' compassion for people was apparent. He was showing us what was really important.

Next He encounters two blind men and a demon-possessed man. These were people who could not be helped by anyone other than Jesus Christ. The same is true today; we have problems that no one else can help us with except Jesus.

Highlights from this Read: I wonder if it was coincidence that the synagogue leader's daughter was twelve and the lady who touched Jesus' cloak had been bleeding for twelve years.

The father of the twelve year old girl in this story is named Jairus. We know this from reading Mark's account. Jairus was the synagogue leader in Capernaum. This is important because in chapter eight we were introduced to the Centurion who had great faith. If you remember, he built the synagogue in Capernaum. Im sure the builder of the synagogue and the leader of the synagogue knew each other. Jairus may have even met Jesus before. In Luke 7:3-6 we read that some of the elders of this synagogue went to Jesus on the Centurion's behalf. Jairus could have been part of this group that went and witnessed Jesus' miraculous healing of the Centurion's servant. Even if he was not part of this group, I have no doubt he knew the Centurion and had heard the story of how Jesus healed his servant without even seeing him. When Jairus' daughter became ill, I'm sure he became desperate. I would. Did the Centurion tell him to go seek out Jesus? It makes me wonder.

Investigation (Resources): Mark 5:22-43 and Luke 8:41-56

Officer Safety (Principles for the LEO to live by): We have to be desperate for Christ but not just in crisis situations. We have to live a life that is desperate for Him all of the time.

Matthew 9:35-38

Briefing: Does your agency have a mission statement? Is it clearly stated where all officers in your agency know what it is? Does it have significance for you and how you do your job?

Dispatch/Assignment:
Review your agencies mission statement. Read Matthew 9:35-38.

On the Street: The definition of mission statement is: a brief description of a company's fundamental purpose. A mission statement answers the question, "Why do we exist?" As you review your agencies mission statement does it describe the purpose of why your agency exists? Does it contain words like, "to protect and serve"?

In this passage we see Jesus' mission statement. I can't take credit for knowing this because I was looking through my grandmother's Bible after she passed away and noticed her hand written note in the margin of Matthew 9:35. It simply said, "Jesus' Mission Statement". Had I not seen her note I would have never realized that Jesus had a mission statement long before corporate America coined the phrase.

While Jesus was on this earth His mission was to teach, preach and heal. This mission and His ultimate purpose were two different things. In verse thirty-five we see His mission statement and in verse thirty-six we see the foreshadowing of His ultimate purpose. Jesus was not only the shepherd who came for us, His sheep, but He came to be the sacrificial lamb that died for all of our sins.

The shepherds of the people Jesus is referring too are the leaders who wanted Him dead. They were leading the people astray. Jesus came to be the Good Shepherd who cared for the flock.

The last two verses in this passage are just as important as the first two. Here Jesus gives us our assignment. Pray for God to send workers out into HIS field. In John 4:35 Jesus tells His disciples to look at the fields because, "They are ripe for the harvest". He goes on to tell them, and us, "I sent you to reap". It's time to go to work.

<u>Highlights from this Read:</u> All four verses are the highlight. In this small section of Matthew we see Jesus' mission statement, His purpose, and our calling.

One thing we don't see much of, but had to have been a very important part of the disciples three years with Jesus was the teaching. There were probably times when they all got together and Jesus explained life and love to them. We obviously don't have a journal of all the time they spent with Him, we only see snapshots of significant events. John 21:25 tells us, "Jesus did many other things as well. If every one of them were written down, I suppose that even the whole world would not have room for the books that would be written."

Can you imagine getting to travel with Him, to study Him, to listen to Him. Luke 10:24 says, "For I tell you that many prophets and kings wanted to see what you see but did not see it, and to hear what you hear but did not hear it." I am in that category of being one of those who want that!

<u>Investigation (Resources):</u> For more reading about Jesus as the good shepherd read John chapter 10 and Psalm 23.

<u>Officer Safety (Principles for the LEO to live by):</u> Jesus showed us His mission statement, now it's time for us to develop ours. The harvest is plentiful but the workers are few.

Matthew 10

Briefing: Do you have briefings in your agency? When I worked for Dallas PD I remember briefings as very structured, informative, and serious. We were expected to be there on time and ready for duty. You did not joke around during briefing.

Dispatch/Assignment:
What kind of information is covered in your briefings? Read Matthew chapter 10.

On the Street: I played football in high school. During football season we always had a briefing before practice. At the time I did not know it was a briefing, the coaches called it a "skull session". I'm still not sure what skull session means but it sure sounded cool.

Jesus is about to send His disciples out into the field. Before they go, He briefs them. He tells them what their assignments are and what authority they have to do these things. He gives them some very specific parameters.

As we read this passage Jesus gives His guys instruction on where to go, what assignments to carry out and what equipment to take. I can relate to this. There are times in our careers when our supervisors have to give us specific assignments. The information they give can be vital to the assignment. Specifics can make the difference between success and failure, life and death.

As a rookie, I wanted to chase dopers all day. There were times when my sergeant would have to give me a specific assignment. Looking back on my rookie years, I realize that at times I lacked focus. At times my sergeant had to step in and assist in directing my focus to areas of my job that I was neglecting. Jesus provides focus through specific instruction.

I like the part in verse sixteen when Jesus tells them to be as shrewd as snakes and as innocent as doves. Isn't this how LEO's are to act? We have to know where and how crimes are being committed (shrewd as snakes). On the flip side we are to have the kind of character that we should never know where or how these things happen because we don't go there or do them (as innocent as doves).

Highlights from this Read: Verse twenty-eight is something every person should ask themselves before considering a job in law enforcement. This is a basic, foundational question that is at the very heart of what we do, putting our lives on the line to protect and serve the people of our jurisdictions. Have you made peace with the one who can kill the body and the soul? You need to because in this job there is a chance you may run across those who want to kill the body but have no control over your soul.

Verse thirty-two is also foundational and vitally important to our entry into heaven. Are you ashamed of God? Do you hide the fact that you are a Christian from your fellow LEOs? Jesus tells us that we are His sheep. I don't want Him to disown me when it comes time to stand before God.

Verse thirty-four mentions peace. As peace officers I feel it is important for us to understand that there will not be peace in the world until Christ returns. The Holy Spirit works through us to keep a semblance of peace here on earth until Christ returns.

Investigation (Resources): Luke's gospel also speaks to standing up for Christ in verses 12:8-9. For more on the peace that Jesus gives read Luke 12:51-53.

Officer Safety (Principles for the LEO to live by): The briefing Jesus gives has eternal implications. Study it and KNOW what He expects of you. It's a matter of life *after* death.

Matthew 11:1-19

Dispatch/Assignment:
Review what you know about John the Baptist. Read Matthew 11:1-19.

Briefing: Have you ever projected your expectations on a leader then been disappointed when they did not turn out to be what you wanted? Usually this is not because of anything they did or did not do but because of our misunderstanding of what we thought they were going to be.

<u>On the Street:</u> John the Baptist is a character that deserves our attention. We know that John the Baptist had disciples. One of Jesus' disciples used to be a disciple of John. In John 1:40 we see that Andrew, Peter's brother, and one of Jesus' twelve, was following John the Baptist when he was told about Jesus.

Jesus says some pretty incredible things about John the Baptist. Jesus tells a crowd of people that "among those born of women there has not risen anyone greater than John the Baptist". This is amazing because in this list of people born of women it includes people like Moses, King David, Abraham, Noah and everyone since Adam. (FYI: This does not include Jesus who was conceived by the Holy Spirit and was fully man AND fully God.)

As great as John the Baptist was, Jesus says, "yet he who is least in the kingdom of heaven is greater than he". How can this be? If you are in heaven you are greater than the greatest human still on earth.

John the Baptist is still one of the most awesome men born of woman. With this fact in mind, does it surprise you that he still questioned who Jesus was? If you read what John said about Jesus in Matthew 3:11, "…He will baptize you with the Holy Spirit and with fire" you see where John gets mixed up. John did not understand that these baptisms were two separate events. At the time Jesus was on the earth He would baptize with the Holy Spirit. The baptism by fire would come at Jesus' second coming.

If John the Baptist can be as great as he was and still have doubts, it's ok for me to have them too as long as I follow John's example. He had doubts but he asked Jesus to clarify. When I have doubts I too need to go to Jesus to clarify. How do I do this since I can't just send one of my disciples, which I don't have, to go ask Him? I pray, read the Bible, and seek counsel from godly men as told in Proverbs 15:22.

Highlights from this Read: John's disciples come to Jesus on the heels of Him sending out the twelve. I wonder if the twelve were around when John's disciples arrived and asked Him the questions. Would it have shaken their faith to see John the Baptist questioning if Jesus is who John thought He was. Jesus' answer should not surprise anyone who has spent any time with Him. This was a fulfillment of Isaiah 29:18-19, and 61:1-2. John would know this passage and understand that Jesus was the completion of this prophesy.

Investigation (Resources): Luke 7:18-35 has more of John's story. For more verses about godly counsel look up Proverbs 3:12, 9:7-9, 19:20 and Ecclesiastes 4:13.

Officer Safety (Principles for the LEO to live by): Know where to go to ask questions. It is very important to read your Bible and to be plugged into a local fellowship.

Matthew 11:20-30

Briefing: Law enforcement personnel are familiar with warning signs. I am always amazed at how people try to justify that the warning applies to everyone but them.

Dispatch/Assignment:
Warning, there is a fork in the road. Which path will you choose? Read Matthew 11:20-30.

On the Street: Let your light shine! A city on a hill cannot be hidden. Are we being compared to a city here? Is it possible that we could meet the same fate as unrepentant cities?

Let's take a look at some of the towns Jesus mentions. Capernaum was the town that Jesus made His home. This city was compared to Sodom. Sodom was a disgusting city that was known for the vile sexual perversions that took place there, yet Jesus said it would have remained to this day if the miracles were performed there.

When Jesus is pronouncing woes on cities, Bethsaida is one of them. Not everything associated with Bethsaida was negative. Bethsaida is believed to be the site of the feeding of the five thousand. John 1:44 says that Peter, Andrew and Phillip all came from Bethsaida. I can't imagine all people from this town being condemned as a whole and not as individuals. The Bible tells us that we will be judged according to our own decisions and choices.

Have you had an experience with Jesus, maybe even got excited for a short while, only to go back to your old life and old familiar way of living? This is what these cities did. It seemed as if they treated Him like a traveling carnival, just temporary entertainment.

Even though Jesus would have preferred that the people of these cities to give themselves whole heartedly to Him, it was not something He dwelt on. He turned His attention to thanking and praising God. 1 Thessalonians 5:18 the Bible says, "Be thankful in all situations".

Jesus tells us that in order to know God we have to know Him, Christ. John 14:6 tells us that Jesus is the only way to God. You can't just believe in the God of Abraham and be saved. The people of the Islamic faith believe in the God of Abraham but they don't believe that Jesus is His son. If you find yourself in a religion that believes you can get to heaven any way other than Christ Jesus, you are headed down the wide road that leads to destruction.

Highlights from this Read: Do you get weighed down by the struggles and problems of this world? Verse twenty-eight gives us the assurance that we can take rest in Jesus.

Jesus mentioned Korazin. Korazin was a major city in Jesus' day. It was famous for wheat production and was only two miles north of Capernaum.

Investigation (Resources): John 14:6 and Luke 10:13-15.

Officer Safety (Principles for the LEO to live by): If heaven were a big castle, there would be only one door to get in. Jesus is that door, there is no other way in.

Matthew 12:1-14

Dispatch/Assignment:
Read Matthew 12:1-14.

Briefing: Have you seen someone get corrected; causing their pride to swell up? Were they able to swallow their pride and accept the correction or did they carry on and compound their problem? Have you ever know yourself to act this way?

On the Street: The Pharisees did not know the correct interpretation of the law. These guys were supposed to be the experts. Jesus said that they have condemned the innocent wrongly. Isn't this what they did to Jesus?

Jesus is Lord of the Sabbath. In my Bible this title is capitalized which tells me that it was meant as an official title. As Lord of the Sabbath, Jesus has total, absolute authority over what is lawful to do on the Sabbath.

Jesus could have easily told them of His authority and walked away, not caring whether or not they understood, but as we have seen so many times before, He has compassion for them. These are the very guys that will plot to kill Him. In our profession, we would call this "going above and beyond". Jesus tries to logically explain but the Pharisees get so hung up on "the letter of the law" that they miss the true meaning. In the passage before this (Matthew 11:25-26) Jesus reveals that God has hidden the meaning from these "teachers" of the law and revealed it to little children, those with childlike faith.

Next we see Jesus in the synagogue healing a man with a shriveled hand. Jesus again is confronted by Pharisees who try to trap Him with the law. Jesus reveals their hypocrisy, knowing that they would have compassion on their animals, but not on this man with the crippled hand.

In this study there are a few sections where we have listed the positive characteristics of individuals. This lesson could be on the negative characteristics of the Pharisees. These leaders were so egotistical that they did not know or care that they were in the presence of God. They saw the miracles He did, just like the cities in Matthew 11:20-24 but like those cities, they were too lost and prideful to change.

Highlights from this Read: Verse six is easy to overlook. Jesus tells the Pharisees that someone greater than the temple is here. It's Him!

For insight on why the Jewish rulers were so absolute in their condemnation of Jesus' work on the Sabbath see the following references. Genesis 2:2 says that Sabbath is on the seventh day of the week. Genesis 2:3 tells us that the Sabbath was holy. Genesis 1:3 tells us about the days and evenings being measured differently than today. Their day started at sundown. Our modern day starts at midnight. Leviticus 23:3, Exodus 34:21, 35:1-3 and Jeremiah 17:21 all speak to doing no work on the Sabbath.

Investigation (Resources): See Mark 2:23-3:6 and Luke 6:1-11 from their perspective. 1 Samuel 21:6 is where you can find the story of David and his men eating the bread. Leviticus 24:5, nine tells of the priest eating the bread.

Officer Safety (Principles for the LEO to live by): As complacency can be a killer in law enforcement, pride can be just as deadly. Be on your guard against spiritual pride. Give Jesus control of your life.

Matthew 12:15-21

Briefing: As members of the Criminal Justice System, do you think that Law Enforcement is winning the war of justice?

Dispatch/Assignment:
Most departments keep crime statistics. Is crime up or down in your jurisdiction? Read Matthew Chapter 12:15-21.

On the Street: Did you know that the profession of Law Enforcement is ordained by God? I believe it is as much a calling as ministry. In verse eighteen we see prophesy out of Isaiah that says God sent Jesus to "proclaim justice to the nations". Towards the end of this prophesy it says Jesus will not quit until, "He leads justice to victory". Jesus was victorious when He rose from the grave!

In this world we still have injustice. 2 Thessalonians 2:1-12 talks about the man of lawlessness that is in this world. Paul, the author of Thessalonians, also tells us that there is something in this world that is holding back the man of lawlessness. Jesus told His disciples in Matthew 5:13-14, "You are the salt of the earth... You are the light of the world". Salt is a preservative. It keeps meat from rotting. It prevents corruption from spreading. Light dispels darkness. It is the presence of the people of God on earth that restrains evil. Our job is to bring Christ to the nations, but He has also called each one of us into law enforcement to be the thin blue line.

Romans 8:28 says, "And we know that in all things God works for the good of those who love Him, *who have been called according to His purpose*". Ephesians 2:10 says, "For we are God's workmanship, created in Christ Jesus to do good works, which God prepared in advance for us to do". Philippians 2:13 says, "for it is God who works in you to will and to *act* according to His good purpose". Ephesians 1:11 says, "In Him we were also *chosen*, having been predestined according to the plan of Him who works out everything in conformity with the purpose of His will".

Romans 13:1-7 tells us about how God has set up every authority. Whoever rebels against authority rebels against God. As law enforcement officers we have been placed in authority by God. The verses above speak of us being chosen. Romans 13:4 says, "For he is God's servant to do you good. But if you do wrong, be afraid, for he does not bear the sword for nothing. He is an agent of wrath to bring punishment on the wrongdoers".

Highlights from this Read: In verse fifteen, "Aware of this" Jesus knew what the Pharisees were plotting to do in verse fourteen so He left because it was not time for Him to be killed. In verse eighteen we see this is also spoken at Jesus' baptism and the Transfiguration (Matt 3:17, 17:5)

Investigation (Resources): Isaiah 42:1-4 is the prophecy of Jesus.

Officer Safety (Principles for the LEO to live by): Work as if working for the Lord because you actually are. If God put you in this position of authority then He is your boss.

Matthew 12:22-45

Briefing: If you are not with me, you are against me.

Dispatch/Assignment:
Have you ever had to take sides? Read Matthew chapter 12:22-45.

On the Street: How do people perceive you? What are your characteristics? If two people were talking and one mentioned your name, what would be the first thing that popped into the other person's mind?

Not too long ago I spoke to an Officer from another agency and told him about a Christian Peace Officer organization of which I was a part. I invited him to one of our Bible studies and his answer was something like this, "I'll pass it on, I know a few officers who are into that kind of stuff". This guy was a nice guy whom I have a lot of respect for but his answer sent chills down my spine. His answer led me to believe that he was not for or against Christ or Bible study. He was indifferent to them. Revelation 3:16 says, "So, because you are lukewarm-neither hot nor cold-I am about to vomit you out of my mouth". That's not a good place to be.

According to Jesus it is black and white, good vs. evil, home vs. visitors. There are no neutral fans; you have to pick a side. Luke 9:26 Jesus tells us, "If anyone is ashamed of me and my words, the Son of Man will be ashamed of him when he comes in His glory and in the glory of the Father and of the holy angels". Again, there is no room for neutrality or timidity.

Years ago Bob Dylan sang a song called "Gotta Serve Somebody". In it he makes many contrasts to who you can serve but when it all comes down to it he says, "It may be the devil or it may be the Lord but you are going to have to serve somebody". Who are you going to serve?

Not getting involved is not an option.

<u>Highlights from this Read:</u> In verse thirty Jesus said, "He who is not with me is against me". It is time to make a choice. In verse thirty-four we ask: How do people define us? Do they define us by what we say or what we do, or both? Most often I don't have the luxury of spending the amount of time it would take to study someone's actions so I have to rely on what they say. Verse thirty-five, a sponge soaks up the things it is placed into contact with. When it is squeezed, the things that were soaked up are the things that come out of it. What pours out of you when you are squeezed? How did all that junk get in there? It takes several squeezes to get all the junk out, be patient. Verse thirty-six through thirty-seven continues this thought of what comes out of our mouth makes us unclean. Psalm 141:3-4 is a great illustration of this thought. Being clean is a foundational step but there is one more thing to do. In verse forty-three through forty-five the Word tells us to fill ourselves (clean sponge) with Christ.

<u>Investigation (Resources):</u> Psalm 141:3-4 is a prayer for God to set a guard over our mouths and heart. Also read Mark 3:23-27 and Luke 11:17-22.

<u>Officer Safety (Principles for the LEO to live by):</u> It is of the utmost importance to choose to serve Christ and then do it in a way that people know where you stand.

Matthew 12:46-50

<u>Dispatch/Assignment:</u>
Read Matthew 12:46-50.

<u>On the Street:</u> I can remember sitting in my granddad's house listening to him and his brother swap stories of the days when they were in the Texas Highway Patrol. The only time I remember them talking "shop" was when it was just the two of them. My granddad was my hero.

Years later I was hired by the City of Dallas to be a Dallas Police Officer. I felt like I was where God wanted me to be.

I quickly realized that LEOs were a different kind of people. They, not yet including myself, were not normal. They had their own language, thought process and views. They only hung out with other cops but when they were around "civilians" they didn't like to discuss the job or tell stories. As I slowly became included in the family (the family of law enforcement) I began to feel some of the same feelings and have some of the same thought processes and views.

Once I was finished with training and riding with more experienced officers, I was assigned a partner. I learned to trust him with my life.

We became best friends both on duty and off duty. I found that I spent more time with my partner and had more conversation with him than I did with my wife.

Most LEOs I know love their job. They may not show it or say it but they have a deep love and respect for their brothers and sisters in the profession. Most of us could never see ourselves in another line of work. With all of this being said, ask a cop if he or she would like to see their children in this job and the answer will be a resounding no!

There is another family that I am a part of that is still very much involved in law enforcement. It is the Fellowship of Christian Peace Officers. We too have a close family connection but ours runs much deeper than I have ever experienced as a police officer. My Christian brothers and sisters in blue have a connection built on Jesus Christ.

In this passage Jesus is not saying that we should not love our earthly family. On the contrary, we should work and pray daily to see them join our spiritual family. The same goes for our brothers and sisters in blue. If we truly love them, we should want them to become part of our spiritual family too.

Highlights from this Read: Jesus tells us we are His brothers and sisters. This is an amazing statement that needs further investigation. See Investigation (Resources) for the verses needed to conduct a self study.

Investigation (Resources): For more on becoming heirs, see Galatians 3:29, 4:7, Hebrews 1:2, Romans 8:17, Ephesians 3:6 and 1 Peter 3:7. Also see Mark 3:31–35 and Luke 8:19–21.

Officer Safety (Principles for the LEO to live by): It's not just a matter of being in the family; it's a matter of where you spend eternity.

Matthew 13:1-23

Briefing: Has anyone ever planted a seed in your life? Maybe it was an academy instructor or field training officer. Can you remember being instructed on something that stuck with you? Whether it was positive or negative, it had an impact on your life and, or career.

Dispatch/Assignment:
Read Matthew 13:1-23, the parable of the sewer.

On the Street: Do you garden? Back in Jesus' day everybody had some experience with fruit and soil. His audience would have understood exactly what He meant. Planting and harvesting was a way of life.

The seed is an incredible thing. Jesus uses it in this parable to describe His message of salvation. Jesus tells us that, "unless a kernel of wheat falls to the ground and dies, it remains only a single seed. But if it dies, it produces many seeds. This is amazing! It has to die before it can become a new life. The same is true for humans. In John chapter three, Jesus tells a Pharisee named Nicodemas that he has to be born again before he can enter the kingdom of heaven. To be born again starts new life which means we must die to our old life. We have to tell Jesus that we are giving our life to Him and we are going to live our new life for Him. This is Jesus' seed.

Back to the parable, this is an explanation of what happens to the seed if we are not careful to take it serious. Do you plant a seed then leave it to water itself and grow on its own? Not if you want it to grow into the plant you hoped it would be.

Our hearts are symbolic of the ground where the seeds are thrown. Jesus is telling us to prepare our hearts so the seed that lands on our heart has the chance to grow roots. Once we have grown roots we have to continue watering (prayer and reading the Bible) the soil so that the roots grow and get deep. The deeper the root the better chance we have to resist getting choked out by the worries of this life and the deceitfulness of wealth. We have to be the good soil.

This is the most important decision anyone can make, the decision to give up this life and live for Jesus. Prepare your heart by prayer and reading the Bible, for this is how you water the seed planted in your heart. This is where you begin to grow roots. The stronger your roots are the more you will flourish.

<u>Highlights from this Read:</u> Can you imagine the crowds that followed Him? They were pushing and pressing in on Him. It's a good thing He could step into a boat.

<u>Investigation (Resources):</u> Read Mark 4:1-20 and Luke 8:4-15 for this parable from their perspective. John 12:24-26 is a good resource on seed and in John 3 Jesus tells us what is meant by being born again and having new life. The mystery can be found in Ephesians 3:6.

<u>Officer Safety (Principles for the LEO to live by):</u> As a cop I was taught, when I go on a call, that death is not an option… for us. Our goal is to go home safe at the end of our shift. This, however, is not true in my spiritual life. I have to die to myself daily. Each day I have to pick up my cross and follow Jesus. In my spirit, death to self and life for Christ is the only option.

Matthew 13:24-30, 36-43

Dispatch/Assignment:
This study skips verses thirty-one through thirty-five but they will be covered in the next study. Read Matthew 13:24-30 and 13:36-43.

Briefing: I'm certain that when you were a rookie that you were given a piece of basic information. Example: culpable mental state. Once you had the basic understanding of this concept your instructor built on it, teaching you how to apply it to the law.

On the Street: In the last study we read about seeds and good soil. In this study we will take this a step further and build on what Jesus has already taught us. In our justice system I have often heard and read, "It is better that ten guilty persons escape justice than to let one innocent person be wrongfully convicted". This is called Blackstone's formulation or ratio. That being said it is actually a Biblical principle. It should not surprise anyone since this country was founded on Biblical principles.

In this passage Satan comes at night. How typical. Most thieves and criminals do their dirty deeds at night, under the cover of darkness. It is also interesting to note that Satan has the ability to plant seeds. He does not plant them to harvest but to disrupt. In John 10:10 Jesus tells us the devil comes only to steal, kill, and destroy. He does not come to plant good or build up.

Why did Satan plant weeds in Jesus' fields? In Matthew 13:7 He said other seeds fell among thorns. Thorns have about as much use as weeds. The weeds will attempt to have the same effect as the thorns, the worries of this life and the deceitfulness of wealth.

We saw how Satan was able to get the seeds that fell along the path, on rocky places, and among the thorns. That wasn't enough for him, now he wants to destroy the seeds that fell on good ground.

We are going to have to endure the weeds until Jesus comes back and takes us home. Until then, we have a job to do. Be the good soil, die to self and become the seed that brings new life.

Highlights from this Read: This passage is closely tied to the previous study. We have been given the information and now have a responsibility to act on it. Once someone knows the speed limit they are expected to obey it.

Investigation (Resources): John 10:10. Contrast this study with the passage in Matthew 25:31-46.

Officer Safety (Principles for the LEO to live by): Be the good soil, die to self and become the seed that brings new life

Matthew 13:31-35

Briefing: Was there a training officer, partner, supervisor, or co-worker who had a significant impact or influence on you?

Dispatch/Assignment:
Think about how much influence you have. Read Matthew 13:31-35.

On the Street: Jesus teaches the importance of influence. Have you ever heard of the butterfly effect? The term was coined by Edward Lorenz. It is part of the chaos theory. The butterfly effect basically theorizes a butterfly that flaps its wings in China could, through the gaining of momentum and outside factors or influences, produce a hurricane on the other side of the world. Wow, I don't give butterflies enough credit.

The example of influence I like best can be found in James chapter three. James is talking about the taming of the tongue and how powerful our words are. He uses the example of a small spark that initiates an entire forest fire. Jesus gives us examples of a mustard seed and yeast. Jesus said the mustard seed is the smallest of garden plant seeds but can grow into a bush so large that it can be mistaken for a tree. He also mentioned yeast that made its way through all of the dough. These are examples of how Christianity will spread across the entire planet.

When you think of influence there is no one in history who had more influence than Jesus. No other leader has inspired so many positive changes in the lives of his followers. Philip Schaff, a historian described the influence Jesus had on the world. "This Jesus of

Nazareth, without money and arms, conquered more millions than Alexander, Caesar, Mohammed, and Napoleon; without science... He shed more light on things human and divine than all philosophers and scholars combined; without the eloquence of schools, He spoke such words of life as were never spoken before or since, and produced effects which lie beyond the reach of orator or poet; without writing a single line, He set more pens in motion, and furnished themes for more sermons, orations, discussions, learned volumes, works of art, and songs of praise than the whole army of great men of ancient and modern times."1★

Highlights from this Read: The Bible is filled with stories of how God took people of little influence and did great things with them. He took Gideon's army and whittled it down to nothing so that everyone would see that it was God who won the battle, not the big army. God wants to be the big influence in our lives.

Investigation (Resources): James 3 is a great chapter on our speech. Also see Mark 4:30-32 and Luke 13:18-21 for other perspectives on this passage.

Officer Safety (Principles for the LEO to live by): Is Jesus the influence in your life?

1★ Philip Schaff, Wikipedia

Matthew 13:44-52

Briefing: If you ask a law enforcement officer what they treasure most, you will get a variety of answers: family, retirement, pension, boats, guns, collections, etc. What is it that you treasure?

Dispatch/Assignment:
Read Matthew 13:44-52. What is your treasure?

On the Street: Treasures and things of great value are the theme of this study. As I thought about this question, I considered all of the things I own. The one physical possession that I value above all others is my old beat up Bible. It has notes and thoughts contained on the pages from years of study that could never be replaced or duplicated.

Many people consider Jesus as their treasure but a deeper study of these verses reveal, we are actually His treasure. We like to think it is us looking for Him when it is actually Jesus who is looking for us. He gave His all for you and me. He bought us with His blood.

If we are Christ followers, we have to live a reciprocal relationship with Him. He loved us so much that He gave up His life for us. We have to demonstrate that same kind of love for Him. Growing up in a Southern Baptist church, I remember singing all of the old hymns. One of my favorites was "I Surrender All". This needs to be our battle cry, I surrender all! Jesus has to be so important in our lives that we are willing to sell off everything we have to be with Him.

Jesus' disciples were mostly fishermen. They would have had a great appreciation for this comparison that Jesus uses of the fish in the net. Even though I'm not much of a fisherman, I understand the meaning of bad fish. This is a picture of judgment.

In the end, Jesus asks the disciples if they understand His analogies of what the kingdom of heaven is like. When they say yes, He tells them one more parable to consider. The disciples, as owners of houses, would have to be able to bring out old and new treasures. Their understanding of scripture and prophesy of Jesus as well as all the new lessons He has taught them. Later Jesus will tell them that the Holy Spirit would remind them of all things He had said to them.

Highlights from this Read: Verse fifty-two ends with Jesus speaking of new treasures. He was their new treasure as in verse forty-four. A good biblical reference of how not to prioritize your earthly possessions is in the story of the rich young ruler. He wanted to follow but not to the extent that he had to sell his earthly treasures (Luke 18:8–30).

Investigation (Resources): Revelation 5:9 tells us that Jesus shed His blood for us. In Matthew 25:31–46 we see the story of the sheep and the goats. John 14:26 is the verse referring to the Holy Spirit teaching us all things and reminding us.

Officer Safety (Principles for the LEO to live by): Jesus gave all for us, we have to give all for Him.

Matthew 13:53-58

Dispatch/Assignment:
Read Matthew 13:53-58.

Briefing: Did you go to academy with, or get hired at the same time as, someone who advanced faster than you? Maybe they promoted before you or got a premium assignment that you wanted? I have experienced this and I resented the guy for it. He turned out to be a really good leader and friend.

On the Street: Webster's Dictionary defines resentment as a feeling of indignant displeasure or persistent ill will at something regarded as wrong, insult or injury.

Who does he think he is coming in here and telling us what to do! Does he think he is better than us? Are you familiar with these statements/questions? As we get older we may not say them as much but we still think them.

This synagogue audience started off being amazed at Jesus' teachings. It almost seems as if they did not recognize Him. They saw the wisdom in what He spoke and taught. They witnessed Him perform miracles. They initially judged Him by His fruit but when they judged Him by whom and what they thought He should be, they became resentful. I wonder if they did not recognize Him at the beginning of His teaching just like the men walking to Emmaus, Luke 24:13-35. In verse sixteen it says, "but they were kept from recognizing Him".

As He continues to teach, it is like the veil is lifted from their eyes and they slowly start to recognize Him as the home town kid. They were doing so well then all of a sudden, someone in the crowd decided to resent the fact that Jesus grew up among them and was now giving them instruction. This scene is reminiscent of what will happen to Jesus in the week leading up to His death. The people of Jerusalem will praise His entrance into the city, five days later shout, "Crucify Him!"

In Mark's version he also mentions that the people were amazed at Jesus, but Mark adds Jesus' amazement at their disbelief. It took a lot to amaze Jesus. The Bible mentions that He was amazed on only two occasions.

<u>Highlights from this Read:</u> The two places where Jesus is said to be amazed are in Mark 6:1-6 and in Luke 7:9.

<u>Investigation (Resources):</u> Mark 6:1-6

<u>Officer Safety (Principles for the LEO to live by):</u> Resentment is a feeling. It comes from a greater sin that is at the root of most of the feelings that get us in trouble: pride.

Matthew 14:1-12

Briefing: As law enforcement officers, we have people attempt to hide the truth from us on a regular basis. Have you ever caught someone in a lie and their pride would not let them admit to it? They would go to their grave holding on to the lie rather than admit the truth.

Dispatch/Assignment:
Does your department have integrity policies? Read Matthew 14:1-12.

On the Street: There are several types of pride. Pride you feel for other people, like your children, when they do good. Pride for a job well done and the negative kind of pride that keeps us from admitting when we are wrong.

How would you define pride? We are going to study bad pride. Webster's dictionary defines this kind of pride as, "proud or disdainful behavior or treatment". I like the descriptions that come out of Proverbs better. Proverbs 11:2 says, "When pride comes, then comes disgrace, but with humility comes wisdom". Proverbs 16:18 says, "Pride goes before destruction, a haughty spirit before a fall".

A while back I watched a show on how hunters in Africa trap monkeys. The hunters would build a sturdy box with a hole cut out of one end. The hole was cut small enough for the monkey to squeeze its hand inside. The hunters would attach the box to a tree then they would place an apple inside.

The trapper would wait for a curious monkey to smell the apple and track it to the box. Once the monkey found the box it would stick its hand in the box to get the apple. Once it grabbed the apple it could not pull it out because the hole in the box was too small. The trapper would then slowly approach the monkey. The closer they got the more frantically the monkey tried to get away. The monkey did not realize that if it would just drop the apple it could be free.

Unfortunately we can be just like the monkey when it comes to our pride. You can see Herod doing the same thing. He knew he should just say no to killing John but instead he let his pride push him around and paint him into a corner.

Highlights from this Read: Compare Herod's sin to Eve's sin in Genesis 3:6 and John's description of sin in 1 John 2:16. In verse six we see Herod's lust and in verse nine we see his pride.

Herod the Tetrarch was the son of Herod Antipas who was the son of Herod the Great. Herod the Great was the king who tried to kill Jesus as a child. He ordered all the children two years and younger killed (Matthew 2:13-18).

Investigation (Resources): Luke 8:3 is good background on how Herod had heard about Jesus. Mark 6:14-29 gives us a little more insight on the story of John's beheading. In verse twenty it says that Herod feared John and protected him, knowing him to be a righteous and holy man.

For more verses on pride see Proverbs 8:13, 13:10, 29:23, and Isaiah 25:11.

Officer Safety (Principles for the LEO to live by): Does your pride control you or do you control your pride?

Matthew 14:13-21

Briefing: "Harsh and Swift" was the banner that hung in our briefing room. It conveyed the attitude we had about the way we carried out justice in our part of the city. Do you know any macho man mentality cops? I do, I was one.

Dispatch/Assignment:
Does your shift or platoon have a slogan or motto that you follow? Read Matthew 14:13-21. What do you think was Jesus' motto?

On the Street: Early on in my career there were two guys on our shift who did something that has stuck with me to this day. We used to be able to go to almost any restaurant or fast food place and eat free. I was told as a rookie that if I ever abused the generosity of the food establishments I would get "set straight" by the other officers in the division. Rumor began to grow about two guys who were going by a drive thru burger joint twice a day, every day. That was abusive. Guys started getting upset at these two for breaking the unwritten rule of restaurant etiquette. When the truth surfaced it was even worse! They were not just going to get food for themselves but at the end of their shift they were getting a second meal to feed some of our homeless. It was bad enough that they were going twice, but now they were feeding the hooks and crooks!

It took a while for me to learn that there was room for compassion in my job. Where did I go from "Protect and Serve" to "Harsh and Swift"? Don't get me wrong, in Romans 13:4 God's word says,

"But if you do wrong, be afraid, for he does not bear the sword for nothing". Sometimes we have to be harsh and swift, but Jesus also teaches us to love and be compassionate.

Jesus had a lot on His plate. His cousin and friend, John the Baptist, had been beheaded. He was attempting to get away for some quiet time. When He gets to the other side of the lake He does not get frustrated because these people won't leave Him alone, He has compassion on them. He wants to care for them and feed them.

Highlights from this Read: Sometimes it is possible to get away and just pray. Luke 5:16 and Mark 6:30-31 are other examples of Jesus looking for quiet places to pray.

Jesus was feeding this crowd spiritual food. The disciples want Jesus to send them away to get physical food. Jesus tells them, "They do not need to go away, you give them something to eat". Is Jesus telling the disciples to minister to them, feed them spiritually? Just like the story of the woman at the well, Jesus told His disciples, "I have food to eat that you know nothing about". Apparently they still did not understand the spiritual feeding.

Investigation (Resources): There are also a couple of other miraculous feedings in the Bible, 2 Kings 4:42-44 and Exodus 16:4. This was said to be a crowd of Jews. Jesus also feeds a crowd of gentiles in Matthew 15:32-38. For different perspectives on this feeding see Mark 6:32-44, Luke 9:10-17 and John 6:1-13. This is the only miracle that is recorded in all four gospels.

Officer Safety (Principles for the LEO to live by): Is compassion one of the tools you have available to you at work or are you only Harsh and Swift all the time? We have to be ready to use either depending on the situation.

Matthew 14:22-36

Briefing: Have you ever gotten that prime assignment, transfer or promotion and took all the credit for getting there? Frank Sinatra had a big hit song, "I Did It My Way". I have been guilty of thinking that way.

Dispatch/Assignment:
Research the internet to see if there are any law enforcement Bible study groups in your area. Read Matthew 14:22-36.

On the Street: Peter's walk is much like my own. I know Jesus is the Christ and I trust Him. Sometimes He leads me to do great things and as long as I keep my eyes on Him, I'm ok. My problems start when I begin to think my success is coming from me. As I begin to fall and come back to reality I remember who I belong to and I cry out.

Peter starts out walking in the spirit by faith. Soon he reverts to his flesh and begins to sink. I imagine it like being at work and having one of those days when walking in the spirit is going well. I am being the person Christ wants me to be and my focus is on Him and obeying His will for me. Next thing I know my co-workers, my boss and people around me start yelling and pulling me down into the crowd and I begin to sink.

It is just like the seed Jesus talked about that landed along the path but fell amongst the thorns. The plant got choked out by the worries of this world and the deceitfulness of life. We are always going to work with thorns at some time in our life and we may have even been one.

I recently met a young man who had enrolled in a local police academy. He asked me if I knew of any police officer Bible studies in his area. I looked and the closest one I could find was in a town about fifteen miles from him. He was so excited to have one that close. He told me he wanted to get his career off on the right foot and was looking for a good Christian law enforcement accountability group. I only wish I had his focus when I started in law enforcement. We can't do this alone. I believe that is why Jesus sent His disciples out in pairs (Matthew 10:5).

Highlights from this Read: Jesus sent the disciples into the storm. Why do you think He did that? Do you think He knew the storm was brewing? I do, I think we are often sent into storms to see how we react. I also think He wants to see how we emerge from the other side. Are we going to be like Sinatra and say, "I did it my way" or are we going to give glory to God?

Some interesting information on the Sea of Galilee. It was known for its quickly developing and violent storms. The sea is 680 feet below sea level and surrounded by hills that rise to 2000 feet above sea level. It is a very shallow lake at only 200 feet deep.

Investigation (Resources): For a different view see Mark 6:45-56 and John 6:16-21. This is the sixth time that they realize He is Christ. See also 7:28-29, 8:27, 9:8, 9:33 and 13:54.

Officer Safety (Principles for the LEO to live by): As we walk with Christ we must keep our focus, but if we lose it and start to sink, refocus on Jesus!

Matthew 15:1-20

Briefing: Have you ever gone home at the end of your shift thinking that our society has reached an all time low? Have you come to the place where you think most people are just bad all the time?

How do you measure how good of a person you are? Read Matthew 15:1-20.

On the Street: Are you a good person? By whose standards do you judge yourself? Who is your measuring rod?

In the Jewish system the Pharisees and the teachers of the law were not only the religious leaders but the lawyers and politicians. They were the heads of the Jewish government as well as the religious system. They were not just the big wigs but the big wigs from the capital city of Jerusalem.

The ultimate Jewish officials were coming down to the much smaller town of Capernaum to deal with Jesus. Can you imagine the egos that were present when they arrived? They would be looking down their noses at Jesus and His disciples. They were there to observe and listen, hoping to catch them violating any kind of Jewish law.

They find, what they believe is, a flaw and confront Jesus. I wonder how long they had to follow Him before they thought they had something? I'm sure they thought they had Jesus cornered like a little kitten, only to discover the Lion of Judah. Jesus responds by telling these leaders of their law breaking. The difference is that the

100

Pharisees and the chief priest were breaking God's law. Man can be held to God's law but God can't be held to man's law. It's a chain of command issue.

We can't get caught up in this way of thinking. We, as law enforcement, are especially susceptible to looking at the criminals we deal with and think that we are better than them. This is flawed thinking and is exactly what Satan wants us to do.

If you insist on comparing yourself to someone, try comparing yourself to Jesus. That is how much we fall short of getting into heaven by ourselves.

Highlights from this Read: The Pharisees and the teachers of the law were from Jerusalem. These were the Big Dogs! They were called in to find fault with Jesus. The Pharisees and chief priests are the weeds of Matthew 13:24-30. They will try one more time to stump Jesus in Matthew 26:59-60. The Pharisees probably don't realize it but Isaiah spoke of them in Isaiah 29:13.

Investigation (Resources): Zechariah 10:2-4 is where we learn what is meant by bad shepherds. Isaiah 29:13 is the verse Jesus quotes in verse eight and nine. Also see Mark 7:1-23.

Officer Safety (Principles for the LEO to live by): The only way for us to be clean is by being covered by the blood of Jesus Christ.

Matthew 15:21-28

Briefing: Did you ever have an experience where you had knowledge of a subject, then you had a life experience that brought it all together in a complete understanding? Example, "Officer I've only had two beers". I had heard it but until I witnessed it I never really believed it.

Dispatch/Assignment:
Do you look for teachable moments in your life? Read Matthew 15:21-28.

On the Street: I believe that the disciples were trying their best to understand Jesus and to "get it". Sometimes we can try too hard and miss the point.

For the most part, the disciples wanted to please their master. In this encounter Jesus gives them another object lesson on faith. It's one thing to hear Him tell them parables about faith, it is quite another to see his teachings lived out by real people.

As Jesus and the disciples were on the road a woman came to Him asking Him to heal her daughter. The disciples were getting aggravated with her persistence. Their reaction did not mimic the example Jesus had set for them. We see them acting more like body guards than disciples. The more Jesus kept quiet the more forceful and persistent she became. They must have felt justified in their actions when Jesus said, "I was sent only to the lost sheep of Israel". That must have made the Jewish disciples feel pretty important.

Then Jesus does the unexpected. He says the woman has great faith and heals her daughter. This must have been shocking to the disciples. Jesus uses the faith of this gentile to show His disciples how far they still have to go in their faith.

They had to be shocked at her understanding of Christ's ability and deity. She spoke with such wisdom and grace, humbling herself to the point of agreement with Jesus when He calls all gentiles "dogs". The disciples had been taught about great faith. She is another example where they see it lived out.

Highlights from this Read: In Mark's version of this passage Jesus was secretly trying to get to Tyre, possibly to defuse the situation. I love the fact that Jesus was controlling the entire timeline. He is like a blacksmith working with the blade of a sword. He will heat it to white hot, and then put it under water to cool it down.

Investigation (Resources): Mark's version can be found in Mark 7:24-30. Luke 18 is a great story of persistence. If you are confused by Jesus' statement about only coming for the Jews, don't be. He had not revealed the secret to them about His coming for all mankind. This can be found in Isaiah 42:6, Ephesians 3:1-13, Romans 1:16 and 2:10-11.

Officer Safety (Principles for the LEO to live by): I would be happy with the scraps from Jesus' table but He has invited us to so much more. We get an invitation to the banquet feast as seen in Matthew 22:1-14. I hope to see you there.

Matthew 15:29-39

Briefing: Have you ever been on two calls that were exactly the same? I have been on thousands and never had the same call twice.

Dispatch/Assignment: Read Matthew 15:29-39 then read Matthew 14:13-21 for the feeding of the five thousand.

On the Street: From a human perspective this would have been a positive movement in Jesus' ministry. Verse thirty-one says the crowd praised the God of Israel. This is significant because these are not Jews, but lost sheep of Israel. This crowd is made up of gentiles. Simply put, a gentile is anyone who is not a Jew. When Jesus fed the five thousand, in Matthew 14:13, it was a Jewish audience.

This is a list of the differences between the two events:

5000 fed
Jewish audience
Started with 5 loaves of bread
12 baskets full of leftovers
The disciples left without Jesus

4000 fed
Gentile audience
Started with 7 loaves of bread
7 baskets of leftovers
Jesus left with the disciples

The similarities are below:

15:19 Jesus gives thanks
15:20 The people were satisfied

14:36 Jesus gives thanks
14:37 The people were satisfied

After the feeding of the five thousand, Jesus sent the disciples on ahead of Him. That is when they ran into the huge storm. "Immediately Jesus made the disciples get into the boat and go on ahead of Him to the other side, while He dismissed the crowd". I wonder if they were having flash backs as they were finishing the feeding of the four thousand. It must have been a relief when, in verse thirty-nine it says, "After Jesus had sent the crowd away, He got into the boat..."

Investigation (Resources): Mark's gospel has this story in 8:1-13.

Officer Safety (Principles for the LEO to live by): In our last study Jesus told the disciples that He only came for the lost sheep of Israel. Here we see that He came for us too. I don't know about you, but I want Him in the boat with me.

Matthew 16:1-12

Briefing: I had a friend once who was a funny, personable, intelligent, charming and charismatic guy. You didn't have to be around him long to get sucked into doing things that you normally would not consider. On the outside he seemed to be the all American guy. On the inside he was full of vile, destructive, hurtful intentions.

Dispatch/Assignment:
Read Matthew 16:1-12, evil influence.

On the Street: As stated in earlier studies, the Pharisees and Sadducees were the "great" men of Jewish society. They were the leaders of the political, civil, legal, and religious systems of the day. If you had aspirations of climbing the corporate ladder in Jesus' day, this would have been your goal.

These leaders would have been the ultimate people of society. I would imagine that any of the disciples would have loved to have the position and authority of the Pharisees or Sadducees. As young children, you would have been taught to look up to and respect these guys.

Jesus knew the hearts of the disciples and gives them a warning in verse six. Don't be sucked into those political, charismatic "leaders". Jesus knew the hearts of the leaders too and did not want His disciples to fall under the influence of the wrong side.

The leaders of Jesus' time were more corrupt than the politicians of our day. That may be hard to comprehend but I believe it's true. They held a lot of power and did not want to relinquish it to anyone, especially Jesus of Nazareth. Jesus knew they would try anything in their power to discredit and embarrass Him and His disciples.

Highlights from this Read: In verse one the Pharisees and Sadducees (the ones from Jerusalem still hanging around) ask Jesus for a sign from heaven. Were the healings, feedings and demon exorcisms not enough? Did they want Jesus to turn the sky green? Jesus was the sign of the times. They just missed it. Compare Jonah to Jesus' own crucifixion and resurrection. Jonah was in the belly of the whale for three days and Jesus will be in the heart of the earth for three days. Not knowing this I can't imagine what the Pharisees must have thought.

I can relate to the disciples in verse seven. I often think with my stomach before I think with my head. Jesus is our daily bread. Jesus seems to be a little disappointed in their response. They still have not come to an understanding that Jesus is Almighty God.

Investigation (Resources): Mark 8:11–21. Luke 12:1 speaks of yeast of the Pharisees being hypocrisy.

Officer Safety (Principles for the LEO to live by): Be on guard for evil influence in your life. It can corrupt quickly and it does not take much corruption to hurt our witness for Christ.

Matthew 16:13-30

Dispatch/Assignment:
Read Matthew 16:13-30.

Briefing: Do you have locations in your jurisdiction that have significant meaning to you? As a young Dallas Officer, my training officer drove me to every location that a Dallas Officer had ever died and told me their names and the circumstances of how they died in the line of duty. Those locations took on new significance for me.

On the Street: If we are not careful it is easy to miss the significance of the location of Jesus' declaration to Peter and the disciples. Caesarea Philippi appears to be the destination of their travels.

Caesarea Philippi was a region of heavy pagan worship. It was a mountainous area that was known for the waters that gushed out of one of the caves in the side of the mountain and the pagan orgies that took place there. Pagans would come to this area, pray to the fertility gods and have sex orgies under the trees on the mountain. They believed that the fertility gods lived deep in the earth and came up through the cave. I don't know about you, but any god that comes from deep in the earth is not a god, but a demon.

I have to think that Jesus was taking the fight to the enemy. He chose Caesarea Philippi for a reason. When churches send out missionaries they don't send them to cities and towns where there are an abundance of churches. They are sent to areas where there is not an opportunity to hear the Word of God. This was a spiritual battleground and Jesus

108

was going behind enemy lines, right up to the enemy HQ to make His stand. Jesus said, "the gates of Hades will not overcome it". The symbolism of the location should not be lost.

While researching Caesarea Philippi I noticed the area directly under the famous cave is described as "bedrock" which translated in Greek means Petra. This is the word Jesus used, in the Greek, when He said, "and on this Petra (rock) I will build my church".

Once they arrived in Caesarea Philippi Jesus asks the question, "Who do people say the Son of Man is?" Why would He choose this place? Jesus says, "On this rock I will build my church".

Highlights from this Read: In verse fifteen Jesus uses His words perfectly. He does not ask, "Who do you think I am?" He asked, "Who do you say I am?" Sometimes what I think about someone and what I say about them are two different things. In verse twenty Jesus tells His disciples not to tell anyone because His time had still not come.

Verse eighteen is very interesting when you look at the original Greek words. Peter, translated from Greek, means detached stone, a single stone. When Jesus says, "on this rock", rock is Petra which actually means bedrock which is many stones. Jesus was saying that on these rocks, the disciples, He would build His church.

Investigation (Resources): Mark 8:27-29 and Luke 9:18-20. Living stones and chosen people 1 Peter 2:4-12. Read Romans 10:14-15, Jesus told them not to tell anyone about Peter's revelation but it was only for a short time. Soon they would be sent out to tell the whole world.

Officer Safety (Principles for the LEO to live by): We need to ask ourselves the same question that Jesus asked His disciples. Who do you say Jesus is?

Matthew 17:1-13

Briefing: Over the years I have been to more training classes, schools and seminars than I can count. I can count on one hand the times someone has told me, this guy knows what he's talking about LISTEN TO HIM. It is usually an indicator that the person really knows his stuff.

well pleased".

Dispatch/Assignment:
Listen to Him. Read Matthew 17:1-13.

On the Street: God is giving His full endorsement of Jesus to Peter, James, and John. This was not the first time God had spoken to a crowd. When Jesus was baptized, Matthew 3:17, God said, "This is my Son, whom I love; with Him I am well pleased".

When I was in college there was an election for the Governor of Texas. It was a political race that I will never forget. One of the men running was an old country boy. His TV ads always depicted him riding a horse with his cowboy hat on. He ran as a "good ole boy" who was going to fix things. His election campaign started out great. He was leading the poles at one time by eighty one percent. He hit a snag on the campaign trail when he made an inappropriate comment comparing sexual assault to bad weather, saying: "If it's inevitable, just relax and enjoy it". He really looked like a great candidate until you listened to him.

The disciples would carry on Jesus' ministry after He was gone. It was important for them to listen to what He was teaching them.

Time was running out and they needed to understand what the gospel was all about.

Highlights from this Read: Peter, James and John were the inner circle. These three were called by Jesus on three separate occasions. (One, in Mark 5:37, when Jesus raised Jairus' daughter from the dead and again in Mark 14:32-36 when Jesus was in the garden of Gethsemane praying.) He asked these three to pray and keep watch with Him. They were close enough to hear His prayers.

The Transfiguration was a singular event in history. Jesus was visibly glorified in the presence of these three select disciples. The Transfiguration was outwardly visible and consisted of an actual physical change in the body, as described in Luke 9:29.

Investigation (Resources): Exodus 24:15-16 is another example where a cloud represents the physical presence of God. For other gospel accounts see Luke 9:28-36 and Mark 9:2-13.

Officer Safety (Principles for the LEO to live by): We have to listen to what the Bible tells us. God speaks to us in that way, among others.

Matthew 17:14-27

Dispatch/Assignment:
Read Matthew 17:14-27. What are you passionate about?

Briefing: Have you ever had a partner who always wanted to talk about his/her favorite subject? I knew a guy who loved a certain theme park and all the movies that this company had made. He talked about it all the time. At times I wondered if this person was born talking about it because that seemed to be all he ever knew.

On the Street: Peter went out with power and authority but could not heal the demon possessed boy. He did not understand why he was not able to perform this act. I like Peter's response, he does not seem to get embarrassed or ashamed, he goes to Jesus to find out why. Jesus does not give him a parable or a riddle. He tells Peter what he lacks.

Later Jesus teaches Peter a new lesson. First, Peter was outside talking to the tax collectors, out of Jesus' hearing. Jesus does something here that we rarely see. When Peter comes inside Jesus reveals some of His supernatural power and answers Peter's question before Peter has a chance to reveal the conversation. I would like to have seen his reaction. Was Peter in need of a little supernatural insight, a little extra convincing?

Jesus explains to Peter that the children of the king are exempt from paying duty and taxes. Jesus is the son of the King of kings. If anyone was ever exempt from paying, Jesus was. I believe Jesus was teaching more than just Peter. John 1:12-13, "Yet to all who received Him, to those who believed in His name, He gave the right to become children of God, children born not of natural descent, nor of human decision or a husband's will, but born of God." We who receive Jesus become sons and daughters and are exempt from paying for our sins at judgment. Jesus Christ paid for our sins on the cross! Not only do we see Jesus paying Peter's tax here, but we see the foreshadowing of Jesus paying for all of us on the cross.

<u>Highlights from this Read:</u> I would like to see the father approach Jesus and kneel, acknowledge Jesus' authority. His request, "have mercy" tells me that he understands God has control of all things, otherwise Jesus would not have the authority to give mercy.

In verse twenty Jesus is telling the disciples that time is running out and they must learn to have more faith. It is also interesting that Matthew is the only gospel writer to include this miracle. Matthew was a tax collector and understood Jesus paying our debt.

<u>Investigation (Resources):</u> Other gospel accounts can be found in Mark 9:14-28 and Luke 9:37-42.

<u>Officer Safety (Principles for the LEO to live by):</u> Judgment is coming, are you a son or daughter of the King?

Matthew 18:1-9

Briefing: Does seniority count in your department? Law enforcement agencies rely strongly on years of service for things such as: requesting days off, promotions, bidding shifts and vacations.

Dispatch/Assignment:
What is your department's policy on seniority benefits? Read Matthew 18:1-9.

On the Street: The disciples had a pecking order. There were, at times, hundreds of people who followed Jesus that considered themselves as His disciples. Out of these, the Bible says that Jesus picked twelve. Of those twelve, we see several times that Jesus has an inner circle of just three: Peter, James and John. Most people would agree that of these three, Peter was the leader.

In the previous study, as in the account in Luke, Jesus had just healed the boy who was demon possessed. His father told Jesus that His disciples could not drive the demon out. I can see an argument of who is greatest between the disciple who could not drive out the demon. One of the disciples probably said something like, "well I could have driven it out". From there an argument could have erupted into the discussion they were having over who was the greatest disciple among the twelve.

Jesus shocks them all by pulling a child out of the crowd and placing the child "among them". They were behaving like children, but not the kind of children Jesus was calling them to be. Jesus contrasts their pride and arrogance against the lowly position of a child. Jesus tells us to quit worrying about our seniority or our place in the chain of command. Concentrate on the things He is teaching you, like putting others first, having mercy and compassion, and follow the example He has been setting for us.

Highlights from this Read: If you are ever looking for an independent study to work on, I would suggest reading Matthew, Mark, Luke and John. While reading the four gospels, look for examples of Jesus correcting the world view of things such as murder.

In verse three Jesus said I must be, "converted". This means to change or turn around. We have to change from what we are, natural human survivors, to what He has called us to be, unnatural, spiritually minded people who think more about dying daily to our self than self survival.

Investigation (Resources): For other gospel accounts see Mark 9:33–37 and Luke 9:46-48. Psalm 116:6 talks about the simple hearted, not the simple minded. I believe Jesus is calling us to be simple hearted like a child.

Officer Safety (Principles for the LEO to live by): Jesus has set the example, we need to follow it.

Matthew 18:10-14

Briefing: How much does Jesus love us? More than we will ever know! Have you ever lost something and gone into a panic because you could not find it? The difference between us losing something and this story is Jesus never loses us, we have a tendency to wander off.

Dispatch/Assignment:
Read Matthew 18:10-14.

On the Street: Jesus is our shepherd. He is talking about the sheep of His flock-us. I used to get really worried about the thought that Jesus would leave me to go look for a back sliding Christian, until I became that back sliding lost sheep. Take comfort in this, in John 10:25-30, we learn that no one can snatch us. It does not say that we are prevented from wondering off, running away or backsliding.

This passage comes after Jesus pronounces woes on those, "Woe to the world because of the things that cause people to sin! Such things must come, but woe to the man through whom they come!" Ouch, we have a huge responsibility to each other, to be a positive, uplifting presence. I can imagine a shepherd getting upset if I try to scare or scatter his flock.

Jesus does not want me to stray. If I stray I am in danger of perishing. If I don't repent, come back to Him, and stay with the flock, I am in danger of perishing. When a shepherd has a sheep that strays too much, he will break one of its legs. He will then keep the sheep with him night and day, nursing it back to health. They develop a very strong bond during this time of healing. This act of breaking the leg has a two-fold meaning. The shepherd and the sheep bond and the sheep learn that straying is not to be tolerated.

Proverbs 3:12 says, "...the Lord disciplines those He loves..." If there was no discipline we would continue to wonder off and perish. Proverbs 5:23 says, "He will die for lack of discipline, led astray by his own great folly".

Highlights from this Read: Verse ten says we have angels who always see the face of God. They are always in His presence.

Investigation (Resources): Luke 15:4-7 is the other gospel account of the lost sheep. Jesus' sheep know His voice and they follow Him, John 10:25-30. Luke 15:11-32 is the parable of the Prodigal son. For more on discipline see Proverbs 15:10 and Psalm 94:12.

Officer Safety (Principles for the LEO to live by): Not only is it important for us not to stray but it is important to make sure that we are not the cause of others going astray.

Matthew 18:15-35

Briefing: We in law enforcement can be real hypocrites sometimes. I spent years working midnights hunting drunk drivers. The guys I worked with were great at finding drunk drivers, writing good reports and even better at testifying in court. The reason some of them were so good was because of their own off duty experience with drinking and driving.

Dispatch/Assignment:
Read Matthew 18:15-35.

On the Street: Jesus continues the thought of us looking out for our brothers and sisters. Not only are we supposed to set an example in our lifestyle but call others out when they mess up. I have a couple of officers at work who are really good at calling me out when my actions don't match up to my words, or when I'm being a hypocrite.

As a Christian police officer I know that non Christian officers watch me at times to see if my actions mirror my words. There are times when I want to let my emotions get the best of me and yell and scream at people I come into contact with while doing my job. It is not easy and some days are better than others.

Brennan Manning says it better than I ever could. "The greatest single cause of atheism in the world today is Christians who acknowledge Jesus with their lips, then walk out the door and deny Him by their lifestyle. That is what an unbelieving world simply finds unbelievable."

Another favorite quote or saying of mine is one my wife tells me, "Your character is who you are and what you do when you think no one is looking".

Highlights from this Read: In the last couple of chapters Jesus has been teaching us how to avoid offending others. Now He shares with us, how to act when others offend us. He tells us that our goal is to win them back, not to argue and prove that we are right and they are wrong. This takes patience, love, self-control (Fruits of the Spirit), tact and prayer.

Verse sixteen is not about who is right or wrong, it is about restoring and reconciliation. The passage goes on to talk about binding things on earth. Jesus is talking about us sinning and the church being responsible for the discipline. This is why people were so afraid of the early churches.

In verse nineteen Jesus refers to His Father in heaven, see Ecclesiastes 4:9-12. In verse twenty-two Jesus is trying to convey that they should keep no record of wrongs as in 1 Corinthians 13:5.

Investigation (Resources): Watch the movie, "Beware of Christians"

Officer Safety (Principles for the LEO to live by): We have to be very careful that the person we portray ourselves to be is the person we really are. We need to be like Christ.

Matthew 19:1-12

Briefing: The national divorce rate is fifty percent. That in and of itself is staggering, but if you look at what researchers say about police officers divorce rate, seventy-five percent, why would anyone who is, or ever plans on getting married, become a cop? A recent study of police suicides in New York turned up even more disturbing news. Of the fourteen most recent police officer suicides, twelve were results of divorce or relationship breakups. Police officers going through a divorce are five times more likely to commit suicide than officers in stable marriages.

Dispatch/Assignment:
Read Matthew 19:1-12 and ask yourself if it is ok for a police officer to divorce their spouse?

On the Street: Divorce. What a hard topic. People are very sensitive to this subject. Everyone I know has been affected by divorce. We all fit into one of these categories: we have had one, our parents have divorced, one or more of our family members has had one, maybe our partner, or neighbors, are on their second or third marriage.

Jesus says, "Whoever divorces his wife, except for sexual immorality, and marries another, commits adultery; and whoever marries her who is divorced commits adultery." We know from the Ten Commandments that adultery is a sin.

Let me ask you a question. When you saw that twenty year old kid drunk and passed out behind the wheel of his car, why did you put him in jail for public intoxication? It was because he was so drunk he could not take care of himself and could have easily been taken advantage of by others. You did it to protect him and the public you serve. Jesus did not come to this earth to make me comfortable. He came to save me from Hell. As a law enforcement officer you have to do things that make others uncomfortable for their safety.

Highlights from this Read: In verse three, the Pharisees ask Jesus a "hard" question. We have not seen the Pharisees since 16:1 when they asked Jesus for a sign. This is a good question because it gives Jesus the opportunity, again, to correct our misunderstanding of life and how God intended it to be.

In verse four, Jesus points them to scripture. This should be a lesson for all of us. How well do we know God's word? In verse seven, the smug Pharisees think they have got Jesus cornered. In verse eight, in the desert, Moses was the people's judge and he made this law for the Jews. It is a man-made-law. In verse nine Jesus sets the record straight. Verse eleven makes me stop in my tracks and think, does our society place too little importance on marriage? How do I know if I am one of the ones "for whom it is given"?

Investigation (Resources): Additional reading on marriage 1 Corinthians 7:1-16, Ephesians 5:22-33, Proverbs 18:22. Also see Mark 10:1-12.

Officer Safety (Principles for the LEO to live by): Our work is cut out for us. We are not given special exception to the rules. We must work harder and trust God more than the civilian when it comes to our marriages. I don't have any short cuts for you except pray for your marriage; work to build it on God's Word and work it out in a way that would glorify our great God.

Matthew 19:13-15

Briefing: Jesus' disciples were not trained in dignitary protection. Even if they had been, Jesus did not want to be treated as such. Here we see the disciples keeping children away from Christ, but with good intentions.

Dispatch/Assignment:
Read Matthew 19:13-15. Are you a child of God?

On the Street: The first thing I see when I read these three verses is not the fact that the disciples kept the children away from Jesus. They thought this was acceptable. Jesus had been healing the lame and the sick for weeks leading up to this. No, what grabbed my attention was when Jesus said, "The kingdom of heaven belongs to such as these". I would have to pull Jesus aside and have Him repeat that one. Lord, what about all of us adults who have given up everything to follow you? Are we not eligible?

What is the greatest gift we can receive? Answer: Salvation. What can we do to earn salvation? Answer: Nothing. It is a free gift from the Lord. We have to accept Jesus' gift of salvation like a child. I once heard it put like this, Jesus Christ offers me the free gift of salvation through His sacrifice on the cross. As an adult, imagine getting a gift at Christmas. When you receive the "gift" do you compare it to the gift you got for the person who gave you the gift? If so, you are counting the cost. That's not a gift. A child on the other hand, accepts a gift without thought of what he/she bought in return for the giver. This is how we must accept Jesus' gift of salvation. I can do nothing to repay Christ.

Am I a child of God? Are you? How do we know? Is it even important?

1) To be a child of God we must be born to God. John 3 is where Nicodemus comes to ask Jesus some questions. Jesus explains to him how we must be born again (John 3:1-21).
2) When we become children of God we receive the Holy Spirit and we become heirs to the kingdom of heaven, just as Jesus mentioned in Matthew (Romans 8:14-17).
3) As children, we grow and mature in our walk with Christ. We have to become obedient to our Father (Philippians 2:14-26).
4) As a child will imitate his earthly father, we must be imitators of our heavenly Father (Ephesians 5:12).
5) Another good word picture of a child growing to maturity in Christ is from 1 Corinthians 3:1-2 where Paul talks of children drinking milk and not being ready to eat solid food. This is found in Hebrews 5:12-14.

Interestingly, I see a separation in the comparison between being a child (flesh) and being a spiritual child, in the aspect of independence. A parent raises a child with the goal that one day they will grow to be an adult and be able to function independently, on their own.

As a spiritual child, we never want to get to a place of independence from God. As a matter of fact we want to grow MORE dependent on Him as we mature in the faith. We strive to trust Him with all that we have.

Officer Safety (Principles for the LEO to live by): Decide to be a child of God today. Time is of the essence.

Matthew 19:16-30

Dispatch/Assignment:
Read Matthew 19:16-30.

Briefing: How tightly are you hanging on to your stuff? I remember getting my first new vehicle. I had only been a police officer for about a year and had gotten to a point where I could afford a new vehicle. It got stolen a month later. I cried.

<u>On the Street:</u> As a general rule, law enforcement officers across the country are not the best paid. When you count the hours spent on academy training, annual in-service, intoxilizer and crime scene certifications, shooting qualifications, annual legislative updates and fitness requirements. It puts into perspective how important it is to keep our skills sharpened continuously. We have as much recurrent training and constant re-certifications as any job out there.

We also have a risk factor to our job that most people don't have. I don't have to convince you that law enforcement is an under paid profession. In this passage Jesus tells His disciples, "it is hard for a rich man to enter the kingdom of heaven". Normally this would not give me cause for concern. However, if you are living and working in the United States of America you are a rich person compared to the rest of the Earth's population.

A quick Google search shows that America is the richest country in the world. America's gross national income is the highest of all countries with Americans taking home $9,708,000,000,000 per year.

The average income worldwide is $7,000 a year. The average US income is $44,000. Like it or not, we are the rich and are susceptible to being the people Jesus is warning. Americans are pleasure driven. We have more possessions and material items than any country in the world.

My son asked me a question the other day. He said, "Dad, if our house was on fire and you only had time to grab one possession, what would you take?" Wow, I have a lot of stuff. I know what my one cherished possession is but I like the other stuff too. What stuff do you have that keeps you from following Christ? What stuff do you do that keeps you from going to church? What stuff occupies your time, money and attention? Do you realize that when we die, all this stuff will no longer be important?

You may not feel like it but you are the rich young ruler. Jesus is asking you to drop everything you are doing and follow Him. It may be in your home, community, or the job or something else.

Highlights from this Read: Notice how Jesus answers the rich young ruler when he asks how to "get eternal life". Jesus tells him what he must do to "enter life". This existence as we know it is not life, it is only a tryout. I want to follow Christ and enter real life.

Jesus said it is hard for a rich person to enter heaven. He did not say it was impossible. Rich people have a tendency to get attached to their stuff. Poor people don't have as much stuff to get attached.

Investigation (Resources): Mark 10:17-30 and Luke 18:18-30. Jesus tells His disciples that with man this is impossible. Philippians 4:13 tells us that we can do all things through Christ! With man it is impossible; with Jesus all things are possible.

Officer Safety (Principles for the LEO to live by): When Jesus asks you to sell everything and follow Him, will you go away sad because you have too much stuff or will you be obedient and follow Him?

Matthew 20:1-16

Briefing: Throughout the gospel of Matthew, Jesus uses parables to show us that our thinking is amiss. Have you ever heard a kid say, "not fair". As a law enforcement officer is there an unwritten part of your job that calls you to make sure that things are fair?

Dispatch/Assignment:
Investigate the issue of fairness and how you apply it in your job. Read Matthew 20:1-16.

On the Street: NOT FAIR!!! I am sure as a child you probably said this phrase a time or two. As adults we still think it but in order not to sound childish, we don't verbalize it. What do you think Jesus was trying to teach us with this parable? Let's pretend for a moment that the land owner is God and the pay is entry into heaven. As we go through this story we see people who were called early in their lives to serve the Lord. They work all their life in the service of God. Later He goes out and hires more workers who are in the middle of their life. They work in the service of the Lord for the last half of their life. He hires still more, some who are in the last days or hours of their life. In the end, all who are hired by God are granted entrance into heaven.

Think of a twenty year old rookie who gets hired by an agency and works until he/she is sixty-two. At the end for their career they get their retirement. Now imagine someone who gets hired on at sixty-one and works one year. At the end of their short career they get the same retirement. Where is the justice in that (not fair)?

126

I know I'm going to heaven because 1 John 5:13 says, "I write these things to you who believe in the name of the Son of God so that you may KNOW that you have eternal life". Now think about the scum bag you put in jail for selling dope to kids last week, who punched you in the face as you tried to arrest him, and has a criminal history of violence against society. On his death bed he is presented the gospel and the Holy Spirit leads him to Christ and salvation. Is it fair that we get the same "pay". He/she gets to go to heaven after the havoc and destructive lived here on earth? Yes.

We serve a great, gracious and merciful God who loves all of His children the same.

Highlights from this Read: In verse seven, by saying that no one hired them, could this be substituted for, "No one ever shared the good news of Jesus Christ with me". In verse eight He gathers everyone around the great throne (see 2 Corinthians 5:10). He begins with the last and moves to the first. Verse thirteen we see that even though He seems to be stern with them, He still calls them friend. In verse fifteen there is a similar answer from God to Job chapter thirty-eight.

Investigation (Resources): Matthew 18:12-14 shows how far God will go for "one of these little ones".

Officer Safety (Principles for the LEO to live by): Beware of thinking you are better than those you are hired to put in jail. We have to be on our guard against a sense of entitlement, being ungrateful or prideful. You never know what plan God has for them.

Matthew 20:20-28

Briefing: We just finished a lesson on fairness. Now we have one of our own trying to jump ahead of us in rank (promotion). Not only does this make us defensive but the way in which they go about it gives us a perceived justification for our reaction (anger).

<u>Dispatch/Assignment:</u>
What is the promotional process for your department? Do you think it is fair? Is it a "good ole boy" system? Read Matthew 20:20-28.

<u>On the Street:</u> Beyond not fair, this is one of our own not playing fair, using unfair tactics. As an officer have you ever been surprised by the uncharacteristic actions of a co-worker? One night, while on patrol, I got in the middle of a gang fight and wound up in the hospital. Some of my fellow officers took my squad car back to the station and put most of my equipment in my locker. When I returned to the job I was short a new pair of binoculars and my personal clip board. I could not believe that another police officer would "take" my stuff. We like to hold our co-workers, especially those in law enforcement, to a higher standard. The truth of the matter is that we are only human, no better or worse than anyone else.

I tend to put the disciples on a higher level. I would not expect this kind of underhandedness from them. One was John, the author of the gospel of John, 1-3 John and Revelation. He and James were already part of Jesus' inner-circle. The only person closer to Jesus was Peter. John's brother James was the first disciple to be martyred (Acts 12:2).

Highlights from this Read: In verse twenty-one, when Jesus asked James and John's mother, "what do you wish?" understand that He already knew what her question was but, He allowed her to ask it anyway. Jesus had already explained to the disciples that He was not going to set up an earthly kingdom. His kingdom would be in heaven and He told them in 19:28 that they would sit on twelve thrones, judging the twelve tribes of Israel. We don't expect this kind of behavior from men who played such a vital role in the beginnings of Christendom. Even though we like to get upset at John, James and their mother, I am awe struck by the remarkable faith they show, believing Jesus was who He claimed to be.

In verse twenty-two, the cup Jesus was referring to was probably the cup of wrath on the cross, Matthew 26:39 and 27:48. In verse twenty-four we see pride and ego, these two ugly beasts that can be traced back to the root of most of our problems. This is usually the root cause of why I get myself into trouble. In verse twenty-seven Jesus turns our understanding upside down.

Jesus gives us the perfect example of servant leadership in verse twenty-eight. We can also read about this in John 13, where He washes His disciple's feet.

Investigation (Resources): The cup of wrath, see 2 Corinthians 5:21, Galatians 3:13 and 1 Peter 2:24, 3:18. Study of Jesus giving His life up for our sins: John 10:11 and 17, 2 Corinthians 5:21, Isaiah 59:20, and Matthew 5:21. Also see Mark 10:35-45.

Officer Safety (Principles for the LEO to live by): We should be careful of our reactions to betrayal. Sometimes our reaction is worse than the betrayal.

Matthew 20:29-34

Briefing: Does a LEO/police officer have the ability to see things that the normal citizen does not? Is it the sight or the skill of observation? Is it just seeing or is it looking for certain things?

Dispatch/Assignment:
Discuss a time when you were off duty, with family or friends, and observed some type of suspicious activity. Did your family or friends see what you saw? Read Matthew 20:29-34.

On the Street: As a rookie I was blessed to have a very experienced and patient Field Training Officer. He regularly observed suspicious activity that never registered in my mind as suspicious. After watching me struggle with my lack of ability to see this he told me, "be patient, you will eventually begin to see things you never saw before". Sure enough, in time, I began to see the things he saw.

Cops have a sixth sense, a special ability to see criminal activity developing that non law enforcement people don't have. This takes time and patience to develop. Likewise the veteran Christian has a spiritual sense that can guide him/her. It is sensitivity to the prompting of the Holy Spirit. Some call it spiritual eyesight. If we are blessed with this special sight we can begin to see things the way Christ wants us to see them.

Here, we see two blind men asking Jesus for their sight. I fully believe that Jesus gave them their physical eyesight as well as spiritual eyesight.

<u>Highlights from this Read:</u> In verse twenty-nine, the great crowds were still following Him. Who do you think made up this crowd: the rich, poor, men, women, Jews, Gentiles, Pharisees, criminals, law abiding citizens, soldiers, or cops? I believe that all walks of life were represented.

In verse thirty, two blind men were sitting by the side of the road begging, when a large crowd approaches them. The most compassionate person to ever walk this earth is in the midst of the crowd. Surely this crowd has learned much from Jesus. They witnessed Him healing the sick and lame and loving everyone along the way.

In verse thirty-two, when Jesus stopped and stood still, everyone that was following Him stopped. Consider Jesus' question and imagine Him asking it of you. "What do you want Me to do for your?" this is what I call a blank check question.

In verse thirty-three, He touched them. I wish I knew how joyful it was for Jesus to see the excitement on their faces, like little children at Christmas, getting the present they hoped for but didn't think they would get. They followed Him. Wouldn't you like to know what happened to these two guys? Were they in the crowd that laid down the palm branches as Jesus entered Jerusalem? Did they shout, "Crucify Him" at the trial before Pilot? Did they become part of the church in Acts?

<u>Investigation (Resources):</u> Verse thirty-three is the fulfillment of Isaiah 42:7 and 42:16. Also see Mark 10:46–52 and Luke 18:35–43.

<u>Officer Safety (Principles for the LEO to live by):</u> Just like the LEO can see criminal activity develop, through training and experience, the Christian will begin to see the pitfalls of sin and temptations as they are forming. This gives us reaction time to pray, prepare to stand and fight, or to flee.

Matthew 21:1-11

Briefing: Crowd control means different things to different agencies. In smaller agencies it could be local parades, school sporting events or local political meetings. In larger agencies it could be professional or collegiate sporting events, concerts, or any number of entertainment venues.

Dispatch/Assignment:
Read Matthew 21:1-11. Think about who makes up this crowd.

On the Street: The crowd is fickle. Have you ever heard of the mob mentality? It's now called "herd behavior" because someone thought that "mob" had too negative of a meaning. We will see, as we get closer to the end of Matthew, a crowd that is easily influenced by the actions of a few. Here we see the disciples start laying their cloaks on the donkey for a seat for Jesus. The crowd soon follows suit and begins to lay their cloaks and freshly cut branches on the path that Jesus is traveling. The next thing you know everyone is yelling and shouting His praises. This crowd quickly gets worked up into a frenzy.

I wonder what the Roman soldiers, who were in the city to keep the crowds from rioting, thought. Do you wonder if they remembered Him three days later when they were beating and crucifying Him? Did any of them say, "Hey, this is the guy that the crowds were praising just three days ago." There is no way that this event could have escaped their attention. Extra soldiers were brought to Jerusalem just for the Passover celebration because of the number of Jews that would be making the pilgrimage to the capital city.

<u>Highlights from this Read:</u> In verse three I have to wonder if the owner of the donkey had already been told, by word of mouth or by dream, that Jesus was coming. Could he have been a friend of Jesus, a follower? Maybe it was someone that Jesus had healed or shown compassion.

Verse four is a fulfillment of Zechariah 9:9. This was important because Matthew was proving Jesus' authenticity through fulfillment of the Old Testament scripture.

In verse five, Jesus predicts the events that will happen in the immediate future. How cool would it have been to hear Him tell you this, then to see it happen!

In verse nine, when the people shouted "Hosanna to the Son of David," every Jew would have understood this to mean that their king had arrived.

The timeline of the events in verse ten was Passover week. There would have been Jews from all over the Middle East, Asia, Egypt and Africa. Historians say that there would have been anywhere from 100,000 to 250,000 visitors in the city during this week. Talk about crowd control!

Verse eleven is a sad statement by the crowd. They missed Jesus for who He really was. They identified Him as a prophet. This is the same crowd that just hailed Him as king "Son of David". They saw Him as king and prophet but missed Him as the promised Messiah or Christ.

<u>Investigation (Resources):</u> Zechariah 14:4-9, Matthew 16:14 (Jesus being identified as a prophet), Matthew 2:23 (prophet from Galilee). Also see Mark 11:1-10, Luke 19:29-38 and John 12:12-15.

<u>Officer Safety (Principles for the LEO to live by):</u> Don't follow the crowd. Make your decision before the crowd has a chance to influence you. Do you recognize Jesus as an earthly king, a prophet of God, or do you see Him for the Savior that He is?

Matthew 21:12-17

Briefing: Have you ever been on a call where there has clearly been some kind of incident but no one wants to talk. I've seen drug dealers shot and no one wanted to press charges or tell who did it because they were afraid of exposing their own guilt in an investigation.

<u>Dispatch/Assignment:</u>
Read Matthew 21:12-17.

<u>On the Street:</u> If we view this passage from the eyes of law enforcement officers our first reaction is that Jesus must be wrong. He is causing a disturbance… right?

Let's take a closer look at what Jesus did. He overturned the tables of the money changers and benches of those selling doves. Why would He do that? I am not qualified to speak for Jesus but I do know what the next verse says. Jesus quotes from Isaiah 56:7 and accuses these money changers and the people selling doves of being thieves. It was not uncommon for the money changers to cheat people with dishonest scales. I have no doubt that was quite a bit of cheating and other corrupt acts occurring.

My next question is this; what do you charge a person with who breaks their own property? There is no charge, this is His house. I think it is so interesting, at the end of this story, when we hear from the chief priest. What is their complaint? It is not that Jesus overturned the tables and ran the thieves and robbers out. As a cop this makes me suspicious. They were upset because children were shouting, "Hosanna to the Son of David". Were the chief priest's in on the cheating scales? Were they getting kickbacks? They were upset because children are claiming Jesus is the Messiah, the Christ.

After Jesus "cleans house", He shows the people what His father's house was meant to be. Jesus shows compassion on the blind and lame. Jesus told us in Matthew 12:7, "I desire mercy not sacrifice" and here, as always, He is being true to His word.

Highlights from this Read: Verse fifteen discusses "wonderful acts". Why didn't the chief priest recognize His miracles as wonderful? Jesus was a threat to the chief priest. He was a threat to their position of power, their livelihood, and the entire religious system.

Verse sixteen mentions "infants" in the sentence. The NKJV calls them "nursing infants". We have seen how all creation cries out to its creator (Isaiah 24:1-13 and Romans 8:18-22), I like the thought that a nursing infant knows God. What happens to that knowledge of God as we grow older?

In verse seventeen we are told that He did not stay in Jerusalem. This reminds me of His birth (Luke 2:7), there was no room for Him. This seems to be an earthly pattern, no room for Christ.

Investigation (Resources): Malachi 3:1 (fulfillment), Isaiah 56:7 (fulfillment of verse thirteen), Proverbs 11:1 (dishonest scales), Psalm 8:2 (verse sixteen), Jeremiah 7:9-11 (the house of the Lord). Also see Mark 11:15-18 and Luke 19:45-47.

Officer Safety (Principles for the LEO to live by): As mentioned in the Highlights from the read, in verse 17, make room in your life for Christ.

Matthew 21:18-22

Briefing: We all know people who can put on a good show. I have a fellow police officer, and friend, who relayed the story of his best friend's father. From all appearances this dad was very normal. One day he was stopped on a routine traffic stop. The officers located a large amount of drugs in the vehicle. It turns out that he had been manufacturing and selling drugs for years and no one knew.

Dispatch/Assignment:
Read Matthew 21:18-22.

On the Street: Jesus was running out of time. He was taking advantage of every teachable moment He had with His disciples. We all know the saying, "you can't judge a book by its cover", but you can you judge a tree by its fruit?

The Jewish leaders looked good on the outside but on the inside their hearts were dark. Jesus will later say to the Pharisees, "You are like whitewashed tombs, which look beautiful on the outside but on the inside are full of dead men's bones and everything unclean" (Matthew 23:27). They looked very religious: pretty leaves. John the Baptist said, "Produce fruit in keeping with repentance" (Matthew 3:8). What good is a beautiful fruit tree that produces no fruit? Jesus warned us about people like this, "By their fruit you will know them" (Matthew 7:16).

Jesus then gives them a lesson on faith. Why are these two lessons together? What does faith and good fruit have in common? I think

Jesus is making a point of telling us where we should put our faith. It is in Him.

There was a man trying to cross a frozen lake. He was afraid that the ice was not thick enough to keep him from falling through. He did not have much faith in the ice. He got down on all fours and began to slowly crawl across the lake. After about an hour he made it to the middle of the lake. Suddenly he heard a loud noise behind him. It was a man on a snowmobile crossing the lake. This man obviously had lots of faith in the thickness of the ice. The first man lay on the ice in terror and watched the snowmobile drive right by him and across to the other side. Six weeks later the same man was going back across the lake. He had a little more faith in the ice than the first time he crossed. As he reached the middle of the lake he once again heard the roar of the snowmobile from behind him. It was also crossing the lake. As the snowmobile got even with him, the ice suddenly cracked, both men fell in and died.

Both of these men had faith in the ice. The first man had a little faith that it would not crack, dropping to an icy death. The rider of the snowmobile had a lot of faith in the thickness of the ice, but also died. The point is not the amount of faith in the ice but where they put their faith. Faith in man is misplaced. Put your faith in the unshakeable, unbreakable, unchangeable Son of the One and only God.

Highlights from this Read: Verse twenty-one Jesus says, "you can say to this mountain, go, throw yourself into the sea, and it will be done". I think of a mountain of problems more than an actual mountain. The key to faith is in not doubting. Jesus says, "I tell you the truth" for a reason.

Investigation (Resources): Matthew 3:10, 7:15-23, 12:33 (fruit), James 1:6. Also see Mark 11:12-14, 20-24.

Officer Safety (Principles for the LEO to live by): 1) Make sure you are not a fruitless tree. 2) Who do you put your faith in?

Matthew 21:23-27

Briefing: In your job as a LEO, have you ever had someone question your authority? If so, how did it make you feel? In my experience, the person questioning authority is usually trying to shake my confidence.

Dispatch/Assignment: Read Matthew 21:23-27. In your agency (local, state, federal or other) who or what gives you authority in your job?

On the Street: In this study, the authority of Jesus is questioned. Who is the highest authority in your agency? Who is the highest authority in your state? Who is the highest authority in your country?

Jesus comes into the temple courts and begins to teach. He is interrupted by the chief priests and the elders. They probably felt like Jesus was on their turf; therefore, He had to give an answer to their question. Their pride flairs up and they ask Jesus, "Who gave you permission to come to our temple and teach?" In their own little way they are calling Him out, disrespecting Him in front of the crowd.

Jesus turns the tables on them. Why would you try to match wits with the creator of the universe? When Jesus responds, I can just imagine their reaction. Have you heard this story? Two people are talking. The first one has a bird in his hands. He puts it behind his back and asks the second one, "is the bird alive or dead?" If the second person says alive, the first person will break the bird's neck and show him a dead bird. If the second person says dead the first person will show him the bird is still alive. The second person is in a no win situation.

The difference here is that Jesus is TRUTH and is not trying to deceive them. The chief priest's problem is that they do not recognize Jesus as Messiah, Son of God. They are not interested in the truth, they want to please the crowd and save face.

The obvious answer to their question is that Jesus was teaching by God's authority. In Matthew 17:5 God tells Peter, "This is my Son, whom I love; with Him I am well pleased. Listen to Him". If there is any question to Jesus' authority to teach, God makes it clear, "*Listen to Him.*"

Highlights from this Read: There is a phrase in verse twenty-three that says, "… the elders of the people". In a democratic government the people are represented by appointed or elected individuals. Unfortunately the people we choose to represent us don't always do a good job. I would not want these elders representing me.

In verse twenty-five wouldn't you like to know what their honest answer is to this question? I don't think they ever stopped to consider what the truth of the question was, only how it would affect them politically.

As to verse twenty-seven, at this point Jesus' answer would not have mattered. They already had made up their mind He was a threat and had to be dealt with. Also, we know it was not time to start the ball rolling, yet. Jesus had a perfect timeline laid out and He still had a couple of days left to teach.

Investigation (Resources): Romans chapter thirteen is where the Christian law enforcement officer gets his/her ordained appointment from God. Also see Mark 11:27-33 and Luke 20:1-8.

Officer Safety (Principles for the LEO to live by): Who is the authority in your life? If your first response is not Jesus, then who/what is it? It is time to submit to His power and give your life to Him.

Matthew 21:28-32

Dispatch/Assignment:
Re-read Matthew 21:23-27, the previous lesson, and continue reading verses 28-32. Think of this as all the same lesson.

Briefing: One thing I have found through years of reading the Bible and exploring different translations is; the chapter breaks do not allow us the opportunity to see the whole story. If you don't pay attention you will miss something immediately before or after your passage. This study builds on the last one. Keep the lessons learned in 21:23-27 in mind while reading this study.

On the Street: Some versions of the Bible place the header "The Parable of the Two Sons" on these verses. This separates it from the previous section titled, "The Authority of Jesus Questioned". In the first lesson we see Jesus ask a question of the chief priests that solicits two responses. Neither response appeals to the chief priests so they decide to answer, "We don't know". This response avoids the truth. In the words of a famous actor, "You can't handle the truth!" I don't think it is a coincidence that Jesus immediately follows this with the parable of the two sons. They were not seeking the truth, they were seeking a politically correct answer.

In the parable of the two sons a father poses the same question to two sons. Each gives an answer, one is an honest answer (like the first discussion the chief priests came up with in verse twenty-five) and the second is a deceitful, wrong answer (like the chief priests' second discussion in verse twenty-six). I believe that Jesus is trying to tell the chief priests, and the crowd, that even if your first response is wrong, it's not too late to come to your senses and do the right thing. It is exactly what the first son did.

Jesus goes on to give an example of sinners who repent, come to their senses, and turn to Jesus. In verse thirty-one, He tells us tax collectors and prostitutes are entering the kingdom of God.

Jesus loved these chief priests and elders of the people. He loved the tax collectors and the prostitutes. He was giving the chief priests another chance to turn and repent. Wow!!! If it were me, I would have written these guys off when they tried to disrespect me in front of the crowd but He is still trying to show them the way to salvation.

Jesus wraps it all up by explaining that John the Baptist tried to show them the way of righteousness but they refused to repent.

Highlights from this Read: In verse twenty-nine, the first son is honest, not deceitful. After saying no he seems to have a change of heart, maybe even a little guilt. In verse thirty, we see the second son either lied or had no respect for his father.

In verse thirty-one, things are not always what they seem. The second son is like the tree with pretty leaves and no fruit.

It is interesting to note, Jesus did not say the priests would not enter heaven. He said they would be last. The first will be last and the last will be first. This thought is seen several places in Matthew, 19:30, 20:16 and 20:27.

Officer Safety (Principles for the LEO to live by): We all make mistakes. If Jesus will give the chief priests, elders, tax collectors, and prostitutes a second chance, we also have a chance. The key is grabbing onto His mercy and accepting His gift.

Matthew 21:33-46

Dispatch/Assignment:
Read Matthew 21:33-46.

Briefing: Do you know when you are beat? Have you ever faced an enemy or foe so strong that no matter what you tried you could not win? I bet you answered "No". As law enforcement we are trained to never say die.

On the Street: There is a movie that came out a couple of years ago called "Gladiator". The main character of the movie was named Maximus. He was a general in the Roman army. His second in command was named Quintus. In the first battle scene the Roman army is about to fight the Germanic tribes of Vindobona. Quintus says to Maximus, "People should know when they are conquered". Maximus responds, "Would you, Quintis? Would I?"

The Jewish leaders were fighting a losing battle. They hate Jesus. They hate Him for all the wrong reasons. Jesus was truth and light, in Him there was no darkness. What does light do to darkness? It exposes it. Darkness cannot exist in the light. These leaders were crooked and corrupt. Jesus was a threat to their way of life.

Every time I read passages like this I ask myself how these Jewish leaders, the most educated scholars of their time, did not realize who Jesus was. I can see that they would lose the battle against Jesus but they could not see. They did not know it (the old religious system) had already been conquered.

142

Jesus was going to conquer death also. Satan wanted Jesus dead. Just like in the parable, in verse thirty-eight, the tenants say, "'This is the heir. 'Come, let's kill him and take his inheritance.' So they took him and threw him out of the vineyard and killed him". Satan thought if he could kill Jesus that all would be his. Little did he know, Jesus was about to conquer death by dying on the cross and saving us from our sin and certain death.

<u>Highlights from this Read:</u> In verse thirty-three, Jesus is still speaking to the elders and the chief priests. These guys should have been extremely familiar with this story. They are the "experts" of Old Testament scripture and yet they did not realize where Jesus was going with the story?

Have you heard the saying, "You can't see the forest for the trees"? What do you think this means? For me it signifies something so obvious that we look right past. How about this, "it's as plain as the nose on your face". As law enforcement officers, what looms so big and obvious in our lives that we don't see it or take note of it?

This parable and in 2 Samuel 12:1-12, Nathan confronts David about Bathsheba but David does not see it coming. Like the chief priests in this story, David answers harshly, passing judgment on himself.

<u>Investigation (Resources):</u> For other gospel accounts see Mark 12:1-12 and Luke 20:9-19. See Isaiah 5:1-7 for more information on the first act of the parable of the tenants.

<u>Officer Safety (Principles for the LEO to live by):</u> Know who Jesus is. Study Him, read about Him, and get to know the one who died for you.

Matthew 22:1-14

Briefing: Sometimes we as law enforcement get to attend some "A list" events. My experience with these kinds of events has always been from the perspective of working them, not as a guest.

Dispatch/Assignment:
Read Matthew 22:1-14.

On the Street: In 2011, I attended Super Bowl XLV. I did not sit and watch the game or the half time show. I was working a security assignment, but I still had fun.

Have you been invited to the party? Are you on the guest list? If our salvation is secure we will get to attend the banquet as a guest, instead of someone working security.

This is an import lesson for us. There are several characters in the story. The first character is a king. He is God, the host. The second character is his son, Jesus. Next are the servants, who are the prophets (Jeremiah 7:25). The last group was those who were invited to the banquet. These are the Jewish people. The poor are Gentiles (a Gentile is defined as anyone who is not a Jew).

All of the people had been invited. They knew there was a banquet coming, but they did not know when. In Matthew 24:36 Jesus says, "No one knows about that day or hour, not even the angels in heaven, nor the Son but only the Father".

Just because the ones who refused to come to the banquet are categorized here as Jews does not mean that we cannot also fit into these roles. See if you could be substituted for one of these characters.

They paid no attention to the Lord's call. Have you been that person who has paid no attention to the things of God? One went to his field and one to his business. The field could be anything from the golf course to the hunting lease. The business is obvious, how many guys do you know that are married to the job.

We get the invitation but the story does not end there. Verse eleven says the King found someone not wearing wedding clothes. Romans 13:14 says, "Rather, clothe yourself with the Lord Jesus Christ, and do not think about how to gratify the desires of the sinful nature." These are the clothes we need to be wearing. He needs to be all over us. We are called to live in such a way that we remind people of Jesus.

Highlights from this Read: In verse eight, the King told "his servant", to go to the street corners and invite everyone. The Jews were God's chosen people but He sent Paul to the Gentiles. I believe "his servant" in verse eight is Paul.

Investigation (Resources): Luke 14:16-24

Officer Safety (Principles for the LEO to live by): Clothe yourself with Jesus so that when you get to the banquet you will get to stay and feast with the King.

Matthew 22:15-22

Briefing: What does the government require of you? Since most law enforcement officers work for a government agency we are required to do quite a bit.

<u>Dispatch/Assignment:</u>
What does your department policy say about religion in the workplace? Read Matthew 22:15-22.

<u>On the Street:</u> The Pharisees have been trying to publicly embarrass Jesus and find fault with Him for months. They must have met and discussed for hours on end how they were going to come up with a way to trip Him up. They have been publicly embarrassed by Jesus every time they have tried to question Him. They could not afford anymore blunders. They must have gotten really excited when they came up with this plan. First they would get someone else to make this next attempt in case Jesus finds a way out of it. That way they could avoid another humiliating defeat.

Secondly, the Herodians where hoping to gain a new ally in the battle against Jesus. The Pharisees did not like the Herodians because they supported Rome. The Pharisees were extreme nationalist, but as the saying goes, the enemy of my enemy is my ally.

They think they have finally devised the perfect plan. Get the Herodians to ask Jesus if the Jews should pay taxes or not. If He says yes, then the Pharisees could paint Him as friendly to Rome and pit the Jews against Him. If He says no, they could turn Him over to

146

Rome as a traitor who publicly told the Jews not to pay their taxes. They must have been really excited about their "fool proof plan".

How do you separate your loyalty to your job and employer from your loyalty to your heavenly Father? Can you be loyal to both? Yes, Paul lays it out in Romans chapter thirteen. I am not just a law enforcement officer; I am a Christian law enforcement officer.

Jesus asks whose inscription is on the coin. When they tell Him it is Caesar's, Jesus tells them to give Caesar what belongs to Caesar. The next question begs to be asked: whose inscription is on your heart? If it is not God, it is time to re-prioritize your life and loyalty.

Highlights from this Read: The Pharisees are beginning to get desperate. Politics make strange bedfellows, is the saying that comes to mind. The Pharisees are teaming up with a hated enemy and this would not be the last time they would find themselves getting into bed with the enemy. Look for them to side with Barabbas in chapter twenty-seven.

Investigation (Resources): For other gospel accounts see Mark 12:13-17 and Luke 20:20-26. Romans 13:1-7 fits this passage like a hand in a glove.

Officer Safety (Principles for the LEO to live by): Jesus wants more than just our loyalty; He wants our lives, so He can save us from death.

Matthew 22:23-40

Read Matthew 22:23-40.

Briefing: Can you imagine how well you would know the law if you had studied it from kindergarten all the way through college. You would be an expert in the law.

Dispatch/Assignment:
See if you can find a training test for your new employees. I challenge you to take the test and see how you do. Read Matthew 22:23-40.

On the Street: The Pharisees, Sadducees and chief priests of Israel started learning the law at a very young age. They would study under a priest as an apprentice. They would spend years memorizing scripture and learning all of the laws of Moses. This was their job, it is what they did full time. They would have known the law forwards and backwards as well as reciting every scripture and prophesy from memory. How is it they missed who Jesus was?

There were forty-eight specific prophecies about the coming Messiah. The chance of one man fulfilling just eight of them is one in one hundred trillion. Jesus fulfilled all forty-eight. The chances of someone fulfilling all of them are one in ten to the one hundred and fifty-seventh power. If you were raised to look for the Messiah and you found a man that was steadily fulfilling them, would you investigate to reveal if he was the one or try to discredit him?

It amazes me how many times Jesus confronts the Jewish leaders about not knowing the law or the scriptures. We see it here, in John 3:10 when Jesus talks to Nicodemus, and also in Matthew 15:3-9,

19:4 and 21:42. Jesus also says they do not know the power of God. This is evident in the miracles Jesus did. Instead of recognizing the power of God displayed in Jesus Christ, they focused on how He would hurt their political standing.

Highlights from this Read: Since the Pharisees failed at tripping up Jesus, the Sadducees thought they would give it a try. They ask Jesus about marriage in heaven. The hypocritical thing about this question was the Sadducees did not believe in resurrection and therefore did not believe in heaven. Maybe they were trying to win Jesus over to their way of thinking. Instead of agreeing with them, He confirms the resurrection and reveals that once in heaven; we will be like the angles. In verse thirty-two Jesus gives them an explanation they could not deny.

The Pharisees take another chance when their disciples fail, in verses 15-17. They ask Jesus to tell them, "Which is the greatest commandment?" In verse thirty-eight He gives them the answer and then gives the second greatest commandment, which is like the first, and can also be found rooted in Leviticus 19:18.

The Jewish leaders thought all of Moses' rules were concrete. They built their religion around these rules. They were so invested in this way of living that they were unwilling to accept new teachings, even if they were from God Himself.

Investigation (Resources): For other gospel accounts see Mark 12:18-31 and Luke 20:27-40. Since both of the two greatest commandments center on loving well, it would be a good idea to read 1 Corinthians chapter 13.

Officer Safety (Principles for the LEO to live by): It is one thing to have head knowledge of the Bible, but if it does not travel the eighteen inches from your brain to your heart, you will wind up being just like the Pharisees.

Matthew 22:41-46

Dispatch/Assignment:
Read Matthew 22:41-46.

Briefing: Have you ever known someone with great book smarts and no common sense. They can be standing in the middle of a rain storm and give you all the meteorological information about the current weather situation, but they don't have the wisdom to get out of the rain.

On the Street: This study builds on the last section. The Pharisees have asked their questions, now it is Jesus' turn. Ok experts of the law and scripture, what do you know about the Messiah? Whose son is He?

"The Lord said to my Lord"
"Yehwah said to the Messiah"
"God said to Jesus"

How is it the two blind men knew who Jesus was (Matthew 20:30) saying, "Lord, son of David, have mercy on us" but these experts did not know? Jesus tells them in His follow up question that David was speaking by the Spirit. Jesus stands His ground and takes every question they have the courage to ask. When they are done, He is the last man standing. His wisdom has stumped them all: the Herodians, Sadduces and Pharisees.

Verse forty-five says, "No one dared ask Him anymore questions". This does not mean they have been convinced that Jesus is Messiah. Their hearts were hardened to the point where they would never understand. They were tired of trying to match wits with Jesus, only to find that His wisdom so far surpassed them, they became humiliated every time they questioned Him. They could quote scripture all day long but they could not tell you what it meant. There was no understanding of wisdom from their knowledge.

<u>Highlights from this Read:</u> In forty-three and fourty-four we see the Trinity. In Psalm 110:1 David writes that the Holy Spirit tells him God was speaking to Jesus.

<u>Investigation (Resources):</u> Mark 12:35-37 and Luke 20:41-44 for other gospel accounts.

<u>Officer Safety (Principles for the LEO to live by):</u> Knowledge of the Word is not enough, we need wisdom and understanding. Read to get the knowledge and pray that God will give you the wisdom.

Matthew 23

Dispatch/Assignment:
Look up the definition of hypocrite. Read Matthew 23.

Briefing: "Forget everything you learned in the academy. I'm going to teach you to be a real cop". These were the famous words of my first Field Training Officer (FTO). My second phase FTO told me, "I'm going to teach you the right way to do things then we are going to do them my way".

<u>On the Street:</u> Jesus has saved us from the law by making the ultimate sacrifice for us so we are no longer under the penalty of law. The law always requires sacrifice, paying the penalty, when it is broken. Even today, when you get caught speeding you have to pay the penalty.

Jesus came along and made it so we never have to pay for our spiritual violations. That does not mean He wants us to go around breaking the law. We are still keeping the law and setting a good example for others.

What areas of your life are you guilty of being hypocritical? The best policy is to be an open book that is truthful. It may be ugly, but at least it is the truth. I would rather be truthful than be deceptive and live a lie. The Bible is black and white with no room for gray. You either live the truth or live a lie. In Revelation 3:15 Jesus tells us to either be hot or cold for the Lord. He hates lukewarm and He will vomit the lukewarm people out of His mouth.

<u>Highlights from this Read:</u> How easy is it for people who rise to positions of leadership to forget where they came from? They seem to hold people under them to a much higher standard than they ever achieved. They lose compassion and mercy. The Pharisees fall into this type of leadership style.

Jesus continues to stress that the people follow their earthly authority. If I were to start my own company, I would want to hire people who would follow my instructions, respect my authority and have a great work ethic. Jesus also wants this. He is always teaching people to live by these virtues and develop these characteristics.

In verse nineteen we see a picture of Jesus leading the people by the hand. They are blind to His teaching. Isaiah 2:3 says, "He will teach us His ways, so that we may walk in His paths". Isaiah 26:7-8 says, "The path of the righteous is level; O upright One, you make the way of the righteous smooth. Yes, Lord, walking in the way of your laws, we wait for you; your name and renown are the desire of our hearts".

Jesus tells us to swear by nothing, just tell the truth (Matthew 5:37). Read verse thirty-seven and compare it to the parable of the vineyard.

Be a God pleaser, not a man pleaser. See Galatians 1:10.

<u>Investigation (Resources):</u> For other gospel accounts see Mark 12:38-39, Luke 13:34-35 and Luke 20:45-46. Look back at Matthew 12:38-39: Pharisees asking Jesus for a sign. For insight on why the Pharisees, Sadducees, chief priests and elders of Israel could not see who Jesus was or hear the truth which came from His words, see Isaiah 6:9.

<u>Officer Safety (Principles for the LEO to live by):</u> Imitation is the sincerest form of flattery. Imitate Jesus.

Matthew 24

Briefing: When I was in high school I was always told that if a police officer was sitting still, running radar, he was required to have his headlights on or he could not write you a ticket. When I was in the police academy studying traffic law, I was surprised to find that my understanding of the law was wrong. It was nothing but an urban legend.

Dispatch/Assignment:
Look for articles on predictions about the end of time. Read Matthew 24.

On the Street: What do you think about the return of Christ? Do you believe we are living in the end times? This entire Chapter is about these questions. It starts off with Jesus making a statement about what will happen to Jerusalem. He says, "not one stone will be left on top of another". This would be fulfilled about forty years later when Rome marched their army to Israel and destroyed Jerusalem. The Roman army literally tore every building to the ground, not leaving one stone on another.

Verse three says the disciples were sitting on the Mount of Olives while Jesus was telling them about the signs of the end of the age and His return. There is no coincidence He picked this location to reveal these things to them. The Mount of Olives will be the very place Jesus returns. Zechariah 14:4, "On that day His feet will stand on the Mount of Olives, east of Jerusalem, and the Mount of Olives will be split in two from east to west, forming a great valley".

I always wondered if I would know when Christ returned or would I be deceived. Jesus tells us that there will be many false teachers and prophets. This chapter gives me reassurance that I will know Him when He comes back to earth. In verse twenty-seven it says that He will come back like lightning and everyone who is prepared will see. We will know. He will come back on the clouds with power and great glory.

Jesus tells the disciples that at the end of times it will be as it was in the days of Noah. One of the things the days of Noah did not have that we still have is the Holy Spirit. If the people of God (those who are in dwelt with His Holy Spirit) are taken out of the world, then it will again be like the days of Noah. Jesus tells us that no one knows when the end will come, not Him or the angles in heaven. Only God knows.

I think it is a fair statement that every generation since Jesus left this earth, has thought they were living in the last days. Our generation is no different. I believe that we have reached the end. I know we cannot know the day or time but I do believe God has revealed the season to us.

Highlights from this Read: Israel has broken its covenant with Yahweh this time by rejecting the Messiah. Jesus will come back on the clouds. Read Acts 1:11 to see more on this.

If Jesus does not know the day or time of His return, then Satan does not know either. Satan has to be ready for the end too; therefore, he always has to have an anti-Christ in place. This would mean there have been several anti-Christs throughout history. We may even have an anti-Christ in place now.

Investigation (Resources): Other gospel accounts can be found in Mark 13:1-37 and Luke 12:42-46, 17:26-27 and 21:5-36.

Officer Safety (Principles for the LEO to live by): Are you ready?

Matthew 25:1-13

Briefing: Are you ready for duty? Some have an extra set of cuffs, some have a backup weapon and I have even seen officers who carry a backup flashlight. I always carry extra magazines, five in all. We all have basic equipment but if it really hits the fan, are you prepared?

Dispatch/Assignment:
Read Matthew 25:1-13.

On the Street: In this parable, Jesus tells us of the bridegroom and the virgins who were waiting for Him. There are three important points to keep in mind.

1) All ten of the virgins knew He was coming, but not all of them were prepared. We, as Christians, have to live a life of preparedness. Just like getting ready for duty every day in putting on your armor and weapons. We have to get up every day preparing ourselves for Christ's return.

2) It is interesting that all ten had their own light. Christians are called to reflect Christ's light. Jesus tells us to be salt and light in a dark world. This light cannot be shared. We have to have our own light. These virgins are in a dark environment and without the light, they are undistinguishable. We are called to be like a city on a hill, letting your light shine for all to see. Don't hide in the dark.

3) They have to cross this darkness to get to the bridegroom. Life is a journey and there are paths that we take. If we walk in

darkness we cannot see which path is the right one. We have to have the light to see where we are going, otherwise we will fall into the pit.

How can we prepare ourselves for this journey? This is a spiritual matter that has to be taken care of in your spirit. As stated above, when you get ready for work, you put on your armor: vest, gun belt, badge and equipment. Spiritually you also have armor to wear. Galatians 6:10-18 lays out the armor of God. This is the battle gear for the spiritual warfare we face daily. Can you imagine going on duty as a cop and not taking your gun belt? How would you perform your duties if you had to arrest a dangerous suspect? You can't do your job without your equipment. The same is true in your Christian journey. You must know and apply the armor of God.

<u>Highlights from this Read:</u> We see in verse five that all became drowsy and fell asleep. I think of the disciples who fell asleep when Jesus was praying in the garden of Gethsemane. Jesus said, "The spirit is willing but the flesh is weak". It is comforting to know that if I do fall asleep, Jesus will wake me at the appointed time as He did with the disciples in the garden and the bridegroom with the virgins.

In verse eleven, the virgins run to the door and call out, "Sir, Sir". Verse twelve Jesus says, "But he replied, 'I tell you the truth, I don't know you'". For insight, we have to go back to 7:21 when Jesus said, "Not everyone who says to me, 'Lord, Lord' will enter the kingdom of heaven, but only he who does the will of my Father who is in heaven'".

Verse thirteen says that no one knows the day or hour of His return. In other verses, Jesus does allude to us being able to discern the season of His return. He tells us there will be a crown for those who look for Him.

<u>Investigation (Resources):</u> Matthew 5:13, 7:21 and Luke 13:24-25.

<u>Officer Safety (Principles for the LEO to live by):</u> I have no doubt you are a wise cop but are you a wise Christian? Are you prepared spiritually?

Matthew 25:14-30

Briefing: Not all law enforcement officers are the same. Some make good supervisors, others make good trainers, and some are good with people. We all have our specialties. What is your unique "gift" or "talent"?

Dispatch/Assignment:
Read Matthew 25:14-30 then write down the gifts and talents you have.

On the Street: Before we get too far in this study, a better understanding of terms will help our application of this lesson. Some translations say the master gave gold. Some say talents or abilities and others say gifts. I believe all of these apply.

Jesus tells us the parable of the talents. As I read through this parable I see the master of the house already knew his people pretty well and gave them assignments according to their ability. He based the amount of talents he would give them on an assessment of their past performance.

Now we move from gifts, talents and abilities to work ethic. You can have all the talent in the world but if you have no work ethic, your talent is worthless. If someone gives you a gift, and you never take it out of the package, what good is it? How much do you get from a gift that you just look at and admire?

What has God put you in charge of? What has He put under your control? How have you been doing with what He gave you? God

158

has put you in a position of authority to meet people's needs. How often do you see people in crisis? What do you do when God inserts you into a particular situation?

We have all been given talents by God. The Bible says you don't light a lamp and put it under a barrel. If you do, you are robbing others of the light. What happened to the servant in this parable who did not use the gift the master gave him?

<u>Highlights from this Read:</u> In verse twenty-five we see the servant hide his talent in the ground. Was this out of fear or just an excuse? The servant who hid the talent did not really know his master. It is amazing how many times the Bible says, "Don't be afraid", Genesis 26:24, Deuteronomy 1:21, 1:29, 20:3, Joshua 1:9, Isaiah 12:2, 44:8, Psalm 56:3-4, Proverbs 3:24 and Mark 5:36.

<u>Investigation (Resources):</u> For more on gifts see Romans 12:4-8 and 1 Corinthians 7:7. Luke 13:24-25 is another gospel account you can review.

<u>Officer Safety (Principles for the LEO to live by):</u> Take a personal inventory of your gifts and talents, and then check yourself to see how you are using them.

Matthew 25:31-46

Dispatch/Assignment:
Read Matthew 25:31-46.

Briefing: Serving as a law enforcement officer, we often come into contact with drug addicts, people with serious health problems, mental illness and worse. These are usually the people the rest of society likes to believe doesn't exist, at least not in their world. We know they exist, we know them by name.

On the Street: I am blessed to be a part of a great spirit led church called "Cottonwood". We are a small country church a few miles outside of the town I live in, population around three thousand which serves from four hundred to five hundred each Sunday. This church has families that serve in South East Asia, Zanzibar, Indonesia and other areas all over the world. This small church goes to the ends of the earth and carries out the great commission with great zeal.

With all of this serving and going, I know there are people in my church who would love to have the opportunities to serve the people described in this passage. Law enforcement officers, have that opportunity on a routine basis. There have been several times when I could have clothed the helpless, fed the starving, took time to share while at the jail, but I didn't. I missed the opportunities. We can do our job and still serve people. Most of the time, we do a much better job when we are serving.

Have you ever gotten to the point in your career where our definition of community policing was putting your community in jail? I have. Police work is a calling to "protect and serve". Most of us are real good at protecting but not so good at serving.

To be a Christian law enforcement officer, check your fruits/actions. Next time you get called to the wrong side of town to deal with the drug addict, the mental subject, or whoever it is in your town, remember the words of Jesus, "I tell you the truth, whatever you did for one of the least of these brothers of mine, you did for me".

Highlights from this Read: There is an obligation to physically feed the hungry, but there is also an expectation to feed those who hunger and thirst for righteousness (Matthew 5:6). This means sharing the gospel as well as sharing your physical possessions. Matthew 10:40-42 takes this farther and says anyone who receives someone who is sent by God will also be rewarded.

The second group, the goats, seems to be surprised by what they are told. It is much like the reaction of the worker in the field (Matthew 20:10-16). This group would have gladly helped the king, but not some stinky, smelly, homeless person.

Investigation (Resources): Luke 13:24-27 is the only other gospel account for this passage. For more on helping the needy see Hebrews 13:2, Luke 24:13-35 and Acts 20:35.

Officer Safety (Principles for the LEO to live by): We will most likely have more opportunities to serve on duty than off duty. Keep your eyes open for chances to serve.

Matthew 26:1-5

Briefing: You receive information that a drug gang is planning an attack on you because of your recent impact on their "business". Your agency offers you protection, what would you do?

Dispatch/Assignment:
What is the penalty for conspiracy to commit murder in your jurisdiction? Read Matthew 26:1-5.

On the Street: In the chapters leading up to twenty-six we see Jesus doing a lot of teaching. It is like actors when their blockbuster movie is about to be released. They make the circuit with appearances on every talk show in town. Obviously there is a great contrast between Jesus trying to share life and an actor trying to drum up business, but you get the idea.

Some of the people, in the crowds that He had spoken to, were the Pharisees, chief priests and the elders of the people. They were the political giants of their day. Even though they were responsible for the welfare of their people, they were corrupt. Jesus referred to the people of Israel as sheep without a shepherd.

These "leaders" of Israel were afraid of Jesus. They feared He might actually be who He claimed to be, the Christ. If this were true, they would be in danger of losing all they had worked for, being power, influence and wealth. This guy was actually starting to convince many people. His triumphal entry must have really enraged them, not to mention every time they tried to trip Him up with questions. He would wow them and the crowd with His answers.

Reading out of the NIV, they use the word "sly" when referring to how the chief priests and elders were plotting to arrest and kill Jesus. They were nothing but a bunch of mob bosses conspiring to commit murder.

The reason they did not want to arrest and kill Him during the feast was because they did not want to start a riot. This was important because Jerusalem was occupied by Rome at the time. Rome still allowed Jerusalem to handle civil matters using their own system. The chief priests and elders were afraid if there was a riot, Rome would totally take over all aspects of government and they would lose their leadership positions.

Jesus is headed for crucifixion. He even knows it will be during the Passover. The chief priests don't want His death to take place during the feast but this is Jesus' path and no man can change His course. For God so loved the world that He gave His only Son, that whoever believes in Him shall not perish but have eternal life. John 3:16.

Investigation (Resources): Hebrews 12:2: Jesus had His eyes fixed on obeying the Father which meant going through the cross. See also John 3:16-21

Officer Safety (Principles for the LEO to live by): The chief priests and elders were willing to kill Jesus in order to keep their power. What are you holding onto today that prevents you from letting Jesus be the King of your life?

Matthew 26:6-13

Briefing: Have you had the opportunity to be around celebrities, sports figures or politicians? Working at the 8th largest airport in the world I have seen many high profile people.

Dispatch/Assignment:
What does your department do when high profile people make appearances in your jurisdiction? Read Matthew 26:6-13.

On the Street: Have you ever been in the presence of greatness? What do you consider greatness? Sports stars, politicians, actors, musicians or business moguls? What makes someone great? When you compare the greatest of the great humans they don't even come close to being in the presence of Jesus.

Mary of Bethany, not to be confused with Mary Magdalene, was in the presence of true greatness. It is obvious from her actions she knew this although the rest of those present may not have been fully aware. How do we know she was aware of His greatness? She sat at His feet, taking a humble position or a servant's position. She sprinkled oil on His head and washed His feet.

The oil is significant, first because of the cost. The disciples say it was worth over three hundred denarii. That is the equivalent of six thousand dollars. This is a huge amount of money. Why would Mary have had a bottle of oil that cost three hundred denarii? It would appear that this was her life savings, maybe even a family heirloom passed down. At any rate, it was a gift fit for a king.

Secondly, it symbolized preparing Jesus for burial. How did she know? Jesus told them three times He was going to be killed. First in Matthew 16:21-28, second in Mark 9:30-32 and the last time in Matthew 20:17-19. Mary displayed the kind of faith and understanding you would expect from someone who believed what Jesus was saying.

Highlights from this Read: This passage is similar to Matthew 9:9-17 where Jesus was having dinner with Matthew and the tax collectors. Jesus explains that His time here is short and they should celebrate. Mary and the tax collectors are celebrating with Him. Another similarity between the two is that Jesus knows the thoughts of those around Him. These were not the only two instances of Jesus doing this. See Matthew 17:24-27 for the story of Jesus paying the temple tax.

This was the week leading up to Passover.

Investigation (Resources): This story can also be found in John 12:1-8, Mark 14:39 and Luke 7:37-38.

Officer Safety (Principles for the LEO to live by): What are you willing to sacrifice for Jesus?

Matthew 26:14-30

Briefing: There is a retired Texas Ranger who has become notorious for being a hired gun for defense attorneys. Have you ever been betrayed? Unfortunately, everyone who reads this probably can testify to a time when they were betrayed.

Dispatch/Assignment:
Read Matthew 26:14-30. Is there a law against betrayal?

On the Street: I am so excited to write this study. As I am writing, it is 6:55pm on Thursday before Good Friday. The events of this story, the last supper, would be happening around the same time I am putting these thoughts on paper. Jesus shares this Passover meal with His disciples on Thursday between 6:00pm and 11:30pm.

In all of the gospel accounts of the last supper, Jesus brings the betrayal issue up early in the evening. Could it be possible that He did this because Judas was not going to share in the meal because of his decision to betray Christ?

Jesus shared the Seder meal (a traditional meal Jews eat at Passover) with eleven of His disciples. Judas does not stick around to eat with them, thereby not sharing in the breaking of the bread and the drinking of the wine, which symbolized Jesus' body broken and poured out for our sins. No, Judas realized that Jesus knew that he had already agreed to betray Him.

<u>Highlights from this Read:</u> This was Thursday night, the beginning of a grueling several hours of abuse. The last supper starts around 6:00pm. Afterwards they go to the garden of Gethsemane where Jesus prays and is arrested. From there He will endure six trials, three civil proceedings and three criminal trials. He will be beaten, mocked, spit upon, and lied about for fourteen hours. This includes the excruciating pain of being crucified on the cross. He was arrested at 1:00am and died at 3:00pm Friday.

Jesus was betrayed for thirty pieces of silver. This was the price you would pay for a slave (see Exodus 21:32). It was also equivalent to four months of salary.

Jesus makes an interesting statement in verse twenty-four. He says what was written about Him was going to happen. There was no way around it. He was going to fulfill scripture. Jesus continues this thought by saying, "but woe to the man who betrays the Son of Man". Judas' betrayal is predicted in Isaiah hundreds of years earlier. Judas had a choice. God knew long ago what Judas was going to do; therefore, Jesus says "It would have been better for that man if he had never been born".

<u>Investigation (Resources):</u> In Matthew 1:21, we learn the meaning of Jesus' name and mission on earth. Mark 14:10-25 and Luke 22:3-20 are the other gospel accounts of the last supper and Judas' betrayal. 1 Corinthians 11:23-32 is a great explanation of the last supper that we now call communion.

<u>Officer Safety (Principles for the LEO to live by):</u> Are you beyond corruption? Without Jesus, I don't think any of us are.

Matthew 26:31-35, 69-75

Dispatch/Assignment:
Read Matthew 26:31-35 and 26:69-75.

Briefing: Shame, embarrassment, guilt and disgrace are just a few of the emotions Peter must have experienced. Have you ever experienced any of these? Have you lost a friend or been the guy or gal who avoided a friend because of these emotions?

On the Street: Peter was the disciple that stepped up and took the leadership role among the disciples. He was the guy that walked on water. He was the one Jesus was talking to when He said "on this rock I will build my church". Peter got to experience things and see Jesus do things that most people were not privy to. He was part of Jesus' inner circle that saw Him raise Jairus' daughter from the dead, the Transfiguration and being close enough to hear Jesus praying in the garden. Peter was out in front of the crowd. All the disciples and followers of Christ could see Peter at the front. When he puts himself out there and says, "Even if all fall away on account of you, I never will".

Peter would soon realize just how wrong he was. Shortly after 1:00am Friday morning, after Jesus had been arrested in the garden, Peter would deny Jesus three times. Peter was so distraught after realizing what he had done, "he went outside and wept bitterly". By now Peter and the disciples knew of Judas' betrayal. They must have been in shock. Now Peter feels he has also betrayed Jesus. The guilt must have torn him apart.

The great part of this story is what happens when Jesus comes back. Peter denied Jesus Friday morning. Jesus was raised Sunday. During this time I can imagine Peter trying to avoid the other disciples because of his shame denying Jesus. He would have been full of guilt and regret. He probably thought Jesus would not want to have anything to do with him ever again, especially in His kingdom.

<u>Highlights from this Read:</u> Jesus was worried about Peter, falling away because of his shame. In Mark 16:7, the angel tells Mary, "go tell His disciples and Peter". He makes a special point of inviting Peter to return to Him because He loved him and wanted to fellowship with him. It is good to read in John 21:7 when Jesus sees them out on the lake and calls out to them. Peter is told it is Jesus and he jumps in the water with all his clothes on and rushes to Jesus. Fellowship was restored and the commission given.

The Bible documents Peter saying, "never" three times. Here, Peter says, "Even if all fall away on account of you, I never will". The first time was in Matthew 16:22 when Jesus predicts His death. Peter speaks out of ignorance, with good intentions. Peter does not yet realize this was Jesus' purpose. Peter seems to think he can control certain events Jesus has total control over. In John 13:8, Jesus was washing the disciple's feet. This was something slaves did, not something the master would do for the slave. Peter tells Jesus, "No, you shall never wash my feet". Jesus tells Peter, "Unless I wash you, you have no part with me". Again, Peter is thinking in earthly terms and not in spiritual terms. Each time Peter says never, it would appear to be the correct earthly, fleshy response. We have to learn to think in a spiritual mindset. When I was in school I was taught that if a test question had "never" or "always" in it, it was a wrong answer.

<u>Investigation (Resources):</u> The other gospel accounts can be found in Mark 14:27-31, 66-72, Luke 22:31-34, 55-62, and John 18:16-18, 25-27.

<u>Officer Safety (Principles for the LEO to live by):</u> Don't let shame, embarrassment, guilt or disgrace keep you from Christ. He forgives and desires to reconcile and fellowship with us.

Matthew 26:36-46

Briefing: Each one of us has a will. You know the saying, "that child has a will of his own". Hopefully you chose a career in law enforcement because you have a will to do good to others.

Dispatch/Assignment:
Read Matthew 26:36-46.

On the Street: Webster's dictionary describes will as; used to express desire, choice, willingness, consent or in negative constructions refusal.

What is your will for your life? As I think about that question I realize my will changes. It is different now that I am married and have children than it was when I was single. As I get closer to retirement my will changes. The biggest change in my will was when Jesus became the most important thing in my life.

My children have a will. Like the saying above, sometimes their will and my will do not match. They have a tendency to forget I have much more life experience and understanding than they (I forgot that too when I was their age). Sometimes they don't realize I want the best for them and my decisions are based on that desire. They only see it as me being mean or unfair.

When Jesus was in the garden praying, He knew exactly what the next fifteen to sixteen hours were going to be like. He knew the beatings, trials, mocking and executions were just over the horizon. I don't blame Him for not wanting to endure it. He looks to His heavenly Father and asks for this "cup" (the cup of wrath) to pass

Him. He barely finishes the sentence before yielding to God and saying, "Yet not as I will, but as you will", seen in verse thirty-nine. He says it again in verse forty-two and forty-three. He was about to suffer things I will never have to experience, yet He went, because it was His Father's will, He knew His Father's will was what had to be done.

Jesus' attitude needs to be our attitude. My prayer is that if I have to endure uncomfortable things for God's will to be done, then so be it.

Highlights from this Read: The timeline for the events in these passages are from 11:30pm Thursday to 1:00am Friday (Good Friday).

God used the symbol of the cup of wrath to communicate His wrath which He would pour out. This is mentioned in Isaiah 51:22, Jeremiah 25:15-16, Ezekiel 23:31-34, Psalm 11:6 (the NIV leaves out the second part of the verse that says, "And this shall be the portion of their cup"), Revelation 14:9-11 and ultimately Isaiah 53:10.

Investigation (Resources): There are two other gospel accounts of Jesus in the garden. They are in Mark 14:32-42 and Luke 22:40-46.

Jesus would often go off by Himself to pray. This can be seen in Luke 4:2, 6:12, Matthew 6:6, 9:38, 14:13, 14:23, 1 Peter 4:7 and John 17:1-5.

Officer Safety (Principles for the LEO to live by): Ask yourself if your will matches up to God's will. If not, what is in your will that is not what God wants?

Matthew 26:47-68

Briefing: Most rookie police officers start their career on either the midnight shift or the evening shift. They spend most of their time in the darkness of night. This tends to be the most active part of the day for criminals, which makes it the most active part of the day for police too.

Dispatch/Assignment:
Read Matthew 26:47-68. Do you have access to crime stats in your area to determine when the crime rate is at its highest?

On the Street: All the events of this story take place under the cover of darkness. Why do you think they took these actions at night? The chief priests have already said they did not want to arrest Jesus during the Passover celebration. Why the sudden change of heart? I believe the answer lies with the same reason most thieves and burglars do their work at night. It is easier to hide and go unnoticed when you have the cover of darkness.

I got into a vehicle pursuit one night with a stolen car. It was occupied by four kids who had just carjacked it. After a lengthy chase, the driver wrecked out and all four kids bailed. I went after the driver while my partner went after one of the other occupants. I was blessed to have "Air One" (one of the Dallas PD helicopters) following the chase. As I began to jump fences, into back yards and chase this kid into areas that I had never been before, I quickly lost my bearings. I remember jumping a fence in the darkness, not knowing where I would land. All of a sudden, Air One's spotlight lit up the driver, who was waiting to ambush me on the other side of the fence. If Air One had not been there to illuminate the darkness below me, I might not be here today.

Cops carry flashlights and have spotlights on their cars. Our job is to bring light to dark places. In our own small way we reveal truth. We uncover the dark things going on not for good but for evil. 1 Thessalonians 5:4-11 speaks to our call to the light. It goes on to say we are sons of the light, not sons of the darkness.

Jesus says it best in John 3:19-21, "This is the verdict: Light has come into the world, but people loved darkness instead of light because their deeds were evil. Everyone who does evil hates the light, and will not come into the light for fear that their deeds will be exposed. But whoever lives by the truth comes into the light, so that it may be seen plainly that what they have done has been done in the sight of God." The chief priest and elders chose to act in darkness rather than light.

<u>Highlights from this Read:</u> The confrontation and arrest of Jesus in the garden is between 1:00am to 1:30am. Jesus' first trial before Annas and the second trail at Caiaphas' took place between 1:30am and 3:00am.

<u>Investigation (Resources):</u> The other gospel accounts are in Mark 14:43-65, Luke 22:47-52 and John 18:12-24. 1 Thessalonians 5:4-11 is a great passage on light and darkness and our call to serve the light.

John 12:35-36 and John 9:4, Jesus is the light of the world. He tells His disciples, "As long as it is day, we must do the work of Him who sent me. Night is coming, when no one can work".

<u>Officer Safety (Principles for the LEO to live by):</u> Are you living in the light or hiding in the dark?

Matthew 27:1-10

Briefing: Have you ever felt sorry for someone you arrested? Not that they were innocent, but a good person who made a bad decision. Don't feel sorry for Judas, he's not that guy.

Dispatch/Assignment: Read Matthew 27:1-10.

On the Street: We are in the job of finding truth and justice. Our justice system's purpose is to see people treated fairly. When was the last time you looked at the statue of justice? It is a blindfolded statue. The message behind it is people in this country will be treated fairly regardless of race, sex, political affiliation or economic status. This was the concept when the founding fathers laid out the foundation of our nation.

No matter how good your plan is, when you throw humans in the mix, you can guarantee it will be corrupted. Israel also had a justice system. It was very different from ours but still had intentions of being fair. The Jewish/Israeli system had become corrupt. The leaders (Pharisees, Sadducees, chief priests and elders) knew Jesus was innocent. He was not a criminal; He was a political threat. These leaders wanted Jesus dead. They had murder in their hearts which lead to an intentional and deliberate plot to crucify Him.

Judas, on the other hand, seems to regret his betrayal of Jesus. When Judas found out Jesus was set to be crucified he takes the money back to the Jewish leaders and confessed he had "betrayed innocent blood". I have often read this passage and felt sorry for Judas because he shows remorse, but on further examination of the character of Judas, the Bible tells a different story. Satan had a hold on Judas, who never showed a strong commitment to Jesus. In John 12:4-6 we see that Judas was the treasurer and often stole money from the very account he was asked to oversee.

Judas was called the son of perdition in John 17:2, which means the son of destruction. In John 10:10, Satan only comes to kill, steal and destroy. It is not too far of a stretch to say Judas was a son of his father Satan.

Peter also betrays Jesus by denying Him three times the night Jesus is arrested. There was a difference between Peter's repentance and Judas' regret.

Highlights from this Read: The timeline during the Passion Week for this event was 5:00am to 6:00am Friday morning.

In verse four, Judas said he had betrayed innocent blood. The response from the chief priest and elders was an admission of their guilt in murdering an innocent man. They did not argue with Judas that Jesus was not innocent, they simply implied, "we don't care" and "we have Him now".

Investigation (Resources): Zechariah eleven is an awesome prophesy of Jesus' coming. Zechariah 11:12-13 speaks to Judas' betrayal which was predicted. Also Acts 1:16-19 talks about Judas being arrested and taking place to fulfill scripture. The chief priests used the money to buy a field to bury foreigners. This can be found in Jeremiah 19:6.

Officer Safety (Principles for the LEO to live by): Study the week leading up to the resurrection. Jesus' death on the cross was for each of us. All men die but Jesus rose from the dead and ascended into heaven.

Matthew 27:11-26

Briefing: In law enforcement we meet so many people. Some I would like to know more about their story or who they were. Barabbas is one of those characters that I am curious to know more about.

Dispatch/Assignment:
Read Matthew 27:11-26.

On the Street: Jesus Barabbas. Does the name shock you? It did me, the first time I learned who he was and what his name meant. Jesus Barabbas was a criminal.

Satan is the father of lies. He will stop at nothing to distort the truth. The name Barabbas means son of the father. Jesus Barabbas obviously would mean Jesus son of the father. Romans 1:25 is not speaking about this event but the words used in the verse are exactly what I would use to describe this situation. "They exchanged the truth of God for a lie…"

Jesus Barabbas was a leader of sedition, an insurrectionist, a murderer and a thief. He was a guilty man deserving of his punishment. Jesus, on the other hand, was totally innocent and undeserving of any punishment. The crowd chose a murderer over the true King of kings and Lord of lords.

Barabbas had dared to resist the mighty power of Rome and was caught in the act of insurrection. He was probably a zealot, at any case a rebel who had committed murder. The Jews were waiting for the Messiah to come and establish the kingdom by force of arms.

When Barabbas was put in prison he became a popular folk hero and just what the people were looking for in a deliverer. He was sentenced to die and was waiting crucifixion. Not long after, Jesus was arrested, humiliated, and deserted by His friends. Because He had not established the kingdom immediately by force the people felt like He had let them down.

To appease the Jews, it was the custom of Pontius Pilate to release one prisoner a year at Passover. Pilate saw no fault in Jesus and proposed that He be released. When the Jews made it clear they wanted Jesus crucified, Pontius presented them with an option that he assumed they could not refuse. He would give them the choice of Barabbas, which he assumed the Jewish leaders would never accept because he was more trouble for the Jews than anyone else, or Jesus Christ. Annas, the high priest would not want revolt by releasing Barabbas, but he did not want Jesus either. To Pilate's shock and amazement they chose Jesus Christ. Pilot could not go back on his word and released Barabbas. He handed Jesus over to be crucified."

Highlights from this Read: Jesus Barabbas was an Edomite, a descendant of Esau. If you are following the timeline of these events, this occurred between 6:00–7:00am.

Keep in mind that Pilot was not a nice guy. He had killed many Jewish people. In verse eleven Pilot asks Jesus if He is the king of the Jews. In Matthew 2:2 the Maji came looking for "The King of the Jews". Yes He was!

Investigation (Resources): Other gospel accounts can be found in Mark 15:2-15, Luke 23:2-3, 18-25 and John 18:25-19:16.

Officer Safety (Principles for the LEO to live by): The devil is a deceiver and we have to be on our guard against his lies. Pray for discernment in matters of truth.

Matthew 27:27-31

Briefing: I have seen my share of brutality and horrible violence in my twenty-two years as a police officer. With all that I have seen and been witness to, I have never seen anything that comes close to what Jesus had to endure.

Dispatch/Assignment:
Read Matthew 27:27-31 and watch the movie, the Passion (if possible).

On the Street: What Jesus is about to endure in this passage is called scourging. It was a cruel punishment that usually preceded crucifixion. This task was carried out by one to six Roman officers called lictors. They were specially trained in the area of knowing how to beat someone to the point of death without actually killing them, thereby getting the most suffering possible from the victim. They were also trained with the whips. They knew where to strike the body for the maximum pain effect and destruction to the body. These whips were called flagellum. They were short whips with knots tied in the ends of each thong. Bone, metal and glass fragments would be inserted into the knots.

When a person was scourged, their clothes were stripped off and they would be tied to a post. The soldiers would repeatedly strike the victim's back, buttocks and legs with their full force causing deep contusions. Lacerations from repeated blows cut into the underlying muscles and ripped the overlaying skin of the back to the point where it hangs off like ribbons of bleeding flesh. Veins were often torn open causing intense bleeding. If the victim fell unconscious the lictor would check for a pulse to see if they were still alive. If they were alive the beatings would continue unless the centurion in charge thought the victim was near death. The Roman soldiers gave this practice the name "half death". The extent of blood loss may have determined how long the victim would have survived on the cross.

Another devastating injury we don't hear much about is when the soldiers, "took off the robe". This sounds innocent enough until you realize Jesus was bleeding profusely under the scarlet robe. The robe would have been sticking to the open wounds and pulling it off would have re-opened the wounds and been very painful.

Highlights from this Read: This occurred from about 8:30-9:30 in the morning. Scarlet was the color of robe that the Roman soldiers wore. This color was used in Isaiah 1:8 to describe our sins. Another very symbolic item used was the crown of thorns. In Genesis 3:17-18 God curses the ground with thorns as a result of Adam's sin (because he listened to Eve and ate from the tree). Also, when the Roman soldiers mocked Him and went out of their way to be cruel to Jesus, it is a fulfillment of Isaiah 53:3.

Investigation (Resources): For more on this study read Mark 15:16-20. Deuteronomy 25:3 states that a man must not be given more than forty lashes. Therefore, Jesus received thirty-nine lashes.

Officer Safety (Principles for the LEO to live by): It is important to see what kind of torture Jesus went through for us. Would you have endured this punishment? Maybe for a loved one but Jesus endured it for all, even His enemies.

Matthew 27:32-44

Briefing: Do you have someone in your town or jurisdiction that you would call a reprobate? This could be the town drunk, they guy who beats his wife every weekend or the kid who sells drugs. Are they beyond saving?

Dispatch/Assignment:
Read Matthew 27:32-44 and Luke 23:32-43.

On the Street: Jesus was crucified between two thieves. This was a fulfillment of Isaiah 53:12. It is shocking to see how much of these final hours of Jesus' life were prophesied about in the Old Testament, yet the chief priests and elders of Israel could not connect the dots.

Through this study we continue to see example after example of Jesus having amazing compassion for those around Him. I think back to the passage where He finds out John the Baptist, His cousin and friend, was killed. Jesus wanted to go to a quiet place and pray. When He got to that place, there were thousands of people chasing after Him to be healed. Jesus stops what He is doing, forgets about His own troubles and focuses on the crowd.

Luke's account goes into much greater detail about the conversation with the thief on the cross. If you have not read Luke 23:32-43 I would suggest you stop here, read it, and come back to the study.

Here, Jesus is nailed to the cross after being beaten beyond comprehension. He must have been in incredible agony from His wounds and blood loss, yet He focuses His attention on one of the thieves next to Him. Jesus grants Him salvation and gives him words of assurance. I like how Jesus tells him, "today you will be with me in paradise". There was no time to get down off the cross and be baptized. Jesus has the power to save you where you are with just a touch or a word.

Lastly, I want to give credit to the chief priests for finally getting something right. In verse forty-three they are quoted as saying, "He trusts in God. Let God rescue Him now if He wants Him". Jesus did trust in God, if He did not trust Him, He would not have allowed Himself to be crucified.

Highlights from this Read: The study of the wine is very interesting. This cup of wine is also referred to by Jesus as the cup of wrath. See Psalm 75:8 on the cup of wrath and Psalm 69:21 for more on gall in the wine. The word crucify means to put on the cross. I used to think it meant death but it is more of an action like shoot or stab. The prophesy that fore tells of this event is found in Psalm 22:18.

Investigation (Resources): Isaiah 53 is a great prophetic passage about Jesus. For more on Jesus' crucifixion read the accounts of Mark (15:22-32) and Luke (19:17-24).

Officer Safety (Principles for the LEO to live by): Jesus, in the midst of terrible suffering, took time to show compassion on a man that could be labeled as a reprobate by those in his community. This reprobate was still loved by Christ. We need to continue to love those who appear to be beyond saving.

Matthew 27:45-61

Briefing: Are you afraid of dying? Do you know where you will spend eternity? Death is something we all have to face. The human condition is terminal. From the day we are born we are only given so long to live. There is only one cure, Jesus Christ.

Dispatch/Assignment:
Read Matthew 27:45-61.

On the Street: Christ dying on the cross was, and is, the darkest event in the history of man. God is light. When He turned His back on the sin of all mankind, carried by Christ when He drank the cup of wrath, everything God ever created was cast into utter darkness. Jesus hung on the cross for three hours with the sin of man all over Him.

If this was how Jesus' story ended, Christianity would be no different from any other religion. The difference is Christ rose from the dead! The best explanation was given by Jesus Himself in John 12:23-29. Jesus says, "The hour has come for the Son of Man to be glorified. I tell you the truth, unless a kernel of wheat falls to the ground and dies, it remains only a single seed. But if it dies, it produces many seeds." A seed cannot come to life and grow unless it is put in the ground dead.

As soon as Jesus dies, life is changed, life is abundant. The dead come to life and the religious system dies. We see in verse fifty-two the tombs broke open and the bodies of many holy people who had died were raised to life. In the verse above, it says the curtain vale was

182

torn in two. The significance of this is all people have direct access to God through the sacrifice of Jesus.

Last but certainly not least, I believe the Roman Centurion is the first Christian convert. In verse fifty-four his confession of, "surely He was the Son of God!" is a beautiful admission. I equate the Roman soldiers of that time to being the local law enforcement of Jerusalem and any other place they occupied. I love the thought of a law enforcement officer being the first Christian. I may be completely wrong about that but I don't think so.

Highlights from this Read: The events in 27:45–56 occurred between 3:00pm – 6:00pm. Jesus' died on Passover. The Passover celebration required the killing of a lamb to protect the firstborn of Israel. Jesus was the lamb. In verse forty-six Jesus calls His Father, "God". It is the first time in the Bible where Jesus calls Him anything other than Father. Jesus was separated from God as prophesied in Isaiah 59:2.

Investigation (Resources): For other gospel accounts see Mark 15:33–41, Luke 23:44–49 and John 19:29-30.

Officer Safety (Principles for the LEO to live by): Are you a Christian law enforcement officer? If not, now is the time to make your confession about Christ. See the page in the back of this study titled, "Do you know Jesus?"

Matthew 27:62-66, 28:11-15

Briefing: Has anyone ever tried to get you to do something wrong or maybe asked you to "look the other way"? This is the exact opposite of what our job demands. We are traitors to our own system, morals, values and ethics if we cross that line. The thin blue line.

Dispatch/Assignment:
Look in your law books for a definition for official oppression. Read Matthew 27:62-66, 28:11-15.

On the Street: I wanted to put a title on this lesson called, "corruption". The problem is Webster's Dictionary defines corruption as: *to change from good to bad, in morals, manners or actions.* The Elders and chief priests of Israel have been bad for so long that you can't accuse them of ever being good. Corruption is like a cancer. It grows and poisons everything it comes into contact with. I wonder if the soldiers were already corrupt too or were they just desperate for a way out of this problem. I hope it was desperation and not corruption.

The Bible does not say for sure, but there is enough information to believe the soldiers sent to guard the tomb were Roman soldiers. The chief priests made the request for a guard to Pilot who assigned soldiers to the tomb. These soldiers would have been the same ones who beat Jesus and nailed Him to the cross. Once a Roman soldier was assigned to a prisoner, he would be responsible for him until the prisoner had a satisfactory disposition. Death would normally be that disposition but since the request was made to guard the tomb for a couple of days, their assignment to Jesus would still be ongoing.

The corruption of the Jewish system was apparently obvious to the Romans. When they fled from the tomb Sunday morning they ran straight to the chief priests, not to Pilot. This was because the penalty for abandoning your post, as a Roman soldier was death. The Jewish leaders would bend the rules and lie for them because it was also in their best interest. They did not want word getting out that Jesus was the Messiah and all He said had been true.

Highlights from this Read: Roman soldiers were not permitted to sleep on duty or abandon their post by penalty of death. A typical "Roman Guard" was an official title like battalion or platoon. There were sixteen soldiers assigned to a "Guard".

Can you imagine the reaction of the chief priests when they heard about the angel and events that took place? I wonder if they realized Jesus was the Messiah; God's Son? Were they afraid? The Bible says they paid the guards a large sum of money. I wonder if it was more than the thirty pieces of silver they paid Judas.

Investigation (Resources): For information about seals, as the one placed on the tomb, see Daniel 6:17.

Officer Safety (Principles for the LEO to live by): I heard a good saying years ago that is so true, someone that will lie for you will also lie to you.

Matthew 28:1-10

Briefing: There are those who think front line law enforcement and military positions are male positions and no place for a female. What is your stance on females in law enforcement?

Dispatch/Assignment:
What percentage of your department or agency is female? Ask someone who has been in your agency for fifteen to twenty years what the percentage was when they started. Read Matthew 28:1-10.

On the Street: I became a peace officer in a time where there was a changing attitude about females in police work. There were already many female police officers working but they described how hard it was for them to gain acceptance. They stayed the course and proved their worth, making it easier for the next generation to do the job with less hassle and fewer barriers to cross. I came out of the police academy with the attitude that a female could do the job just as well as a male.

My first Field Training Officer was a twenty-seven year veteran of the force. He was a soft spoken man with hard features. He looked like an aged Robert Redford. He did not have much use for female officers and my attitude began to shift with his influence. My next FTO had over twenty years and the same attitude. The third and fourth FTOs did nothing to change my fast warping ideas of female cops. It did not help that I worked in the toughest division of the city and there were no females who worked these particular areas.

After a year of being out of training and working the streets, my section was assigned a new Sergeant; a female Sergeant. You can imagine the talk around the station. Without going into pages of details, she corrected our skewed perception of female police officers. She was smart, forceful, authoritative, confident, and a great street cop.

This brings us to the females in this passage. They lived in a time when women were considered second class citizens and not of much use. Jesus, however, had a different view of the role they would play. He allowed them to be a major part of His ministry on earth and, as we see here, gave the greatest honor to one of them. She was given the honor of being the first human to have an encounter with Him after His resurrection.

Because women did not rank very high in those days, it was a very radical move for Matthew to list five women in Jesus' genealogy. I also find it amazing that the women and the Roman guards were there when the angel appeared; however, the guards were scared and left but the women stayed. That's courage.

Highlights from this Read: In the very first verse of this chapter we are told the women went to the tomb on the first day of the week, the day after the Sabbath. The Sabbath is Saturday. Jesus rose on Sunday. This is significant because the day of worship was Saturday not Sunday. The followers of Christ worshiped on Saturday but they began to celebrate Sunday because it is the day of Christ's resurrection. It stuck and that is why we have church services on Sunday, to celebrate the resurrection of Jesus Christ. Every Sunday is Easter!

Investigation (Resources): Matthew 16:21 is fulfilled in verse six. For more on the women going to Jesus' tomb read Mark 16:1-8, Luke 24:1-10 and John 20:1-8.

Officer Safety (Principles for the LEO to live by): Do not discount anyone's ability to serve in the advancement of the kingdom.

Matthew 28:16-20

Briefing: Who would you say is your ultimate authority? I have a lieutenant over me, a deputy chief over him, a police chief over him, a director of public safety over him, a director of operations over him, and so on. My state has a Governor, my district has representatives for congress and senate, both state and federal. The country I live in has a President, but my ultimate authority is God.

Dispatch/Assignment:
Read Matthew 28:16-20. Make a list of the different authority figures in your chain of command.

On the Street: We have come to the end of an incredible journey through Matthew. I can't think of a better way to end it than discussing who the ultimate authority figure is in our lives.

Jesus begins His ministry with His forty days of temptation in the desert after being baptized by John. At the end of being tempted by the devil/Satan in (Matthew 4:8-9), he takes Jesus to a high mountain to show Him all the kingdoms of the world. Satan tells Jesus he will give Him all of this if He will bow down and worship him. Jesus knows who has authority to give all of the kingdoms of the world. It's God, not Satan.

Satan can come up with some real appealing temptations. Have you ever heard the saying, "knowing is half the battle"? Knowing that Satan is the father of lies, realizing with temptations, you are being offered something that is not as it appears, is a lie. Knowing this will make it easier for you to resist or flee.

Jesus tells the disciples, "All authority in heaven and on earth has been given to me". Who gave this authority to Him? It was not Satan. It was given to Him by His Father, God. Satan pretends to have authority to give you all the stuff you need. God has the absolute authority to give you life and salvation. As we discussed in an earlier study, you have got to choose one or the other, God or Satan. Who will you choose to be your authority?

Highlights from this Read: We can read in Acts 8:16 about how Peter and John follow through on Jesus' commission to them. In verse sixteen it only mentions eleven disciples. We learned in Matthew 27:3-5 that Judas had hung himself.

I love the way Matthew ends his gospel. Jesus is quoted saying, "I am with you always". In the first chapter of Matthew we read that Joseph and Mary were to name Him Immanuel which meant, "God with us". Isaiah 7:14 says, "Therefore the Lord Himself will give you a sign: The virgin will conceive and give birth to a son, and will call Him Immanuel". These are great bookends to the Gospel according to Matthew.

Investigation (Resources): For more on the authority of Jesus read John 17:1-5. Isaiah 8:8 and 10 are a good read for additional verses on Immanuel.

Officer Safety (Principles for the LEO to live by): Make Jesus Christ the absolute, ultimate authority in your life today.

Do you know Jesus?

Briefing: This is by far the most important decision of your life. As a fellow peace officer I am your back up on this call. I can't let you go into the next call or assignment of your life without telling you the risk. There is a murderer waiting on the other side of the door waiting to ambush you and take your life.

On the street: Genesis 4:7, God tells us that, "sin is crouching at your door; it desires to have you, but you must master it". Satan is the father of lies, the deceiver. His desire is to kill you. John 10:10 calls Satan the thief in this verse, "The thief comes only to steal and kill and destroy". There is only one way to defeat Satan and certain death. If you don't have Christ in your life you will die in your sin and will spend eternity in Hell.

To be saved by Jesus Christ the Bible lays out what you must do. Think of it as the elements of the offense for becoming a Christ follower. Romans 10:9, "That if you confess with your mouth, 'Jesus is Lord,' and believe in your heart that God raised Him from the dead, you will be saved."

You must admit you are a sinner. "As it is written: 'There is no one righteous, not even one'" Romans 3:10. There is not one person on this earth who is sinless, who knows this better than a law enforcement officer? We too are guilty of sin that is just a fact.

You must be willing to turn from sin and repent/confess. "In the past God overlooked such ignorance, but now He commands all people everywhere to repent." Acts 17:30.

You must believe that Jesus Christ died for you, was buried and rose from the dead. Romans 5:8 tells us, "But God demonstrates His own love for us in this: While we were still sinners, Christ died for us". Romans 10:9-10 says, "That if you confess with your mouth, 'Jesus is Lord', and believe in your heart that God raised Him from the dead, you will be saved. For it is with your heart that you believe and are justified, and it is with your mouth that you confess and are saved."

Now is the critical point. You have been given all of the evidence you need to convict yourself as a sinner without a savior. No partner, SWAT team or anything else can save you. Jesus is the only way. He is reaching down to pull you out and save you but you have to reach up to Him and take His hand. The way to do this is to pray to Him. Confess your sins to Him, tell Him you believe in Him. Cry out that you need Him and you desire to give up your life for Him. Ask Him to be your own personal Savior and come into your life. Romans 10:13 says, "for everyone who calls on the name of the Lord will be saved."

Officer Safety (Principles for the LEO to live by): This is the ultimate decision in your life. This life is only a testing ground to determine where you will spend eternity. Chose wisely.

Fundamentals of the Faith

Briefing: Aside from any denominational issues and arguments, here are eight foundational beliefs listed I believe are non–negotiables of the Christian faith.

God: There is one God, Holy, eternally existing and manifesting Himself to us in three persons – Father, Son and Holy Spirit. God is merciful and loves us, but is just and must punish sin. (John 14:6 & 10 Exodus 34:6, 7 Matthew 28:19 John 3:16)

Christ: Jesus Christ is God incarnate. He was supernaturally conceived, born of a virgin, was put to death by crucifixion under Pontius Pilate, was raised from the dead on the third day and now sits at the Father's right hand and He is coming again personally, bodily and visibly to this earth. (Luke 1:26:35 I Corinthians 15: 3,4 John 1:1, 2, 14)

Holy Spirit: The Holy Spirit is God. He dwells in all believers, having baptized them into the body of Christ at the time of regeneration. (Romans 8:9 I Corinthians 12:13, 14 Ephesians 4:4, 5)

Bible: The scripture of the Old and New Testament was verbally inspired by God and inerrant in the original writings, and is the supreme and final authority for our faith and life. (II Tim. 3:16-17, II Peter 1:20-21)

Grace: Eternal Life is a free gift and cannot be earned. We are saved by grace and not by our own works. (Ephesians 2:8, 9 Romans 6:23)

Faith: All those who by faith receive Jesus Christ as their personal Lord and Savior and who confess Him as such before their fellow men become heirs of God and joint heirs with Jesus Christ. (Romans10:9, 10 Ephesians 2:8, 9 Romans 8:16, 17 John 1:12)

Man: We are sinners. By His death upon the cross the Lord Jesus Christ made a perfect atonement for sin, redeeming us from the curse of the law by becoming a curse in our place. (Rom. 3:23 John 3:18 Gal. 3:13)

Judgment: Those who reject the love of God and the saving work of Christ will be judged and punished for sin. They will be separated from God eternally. (John 16:7-11 Jude 14, 15 John 3:36)

AFTERWORD

Jesus came to this earth to save us by dying on the cross. While He was here, He taught us how to live so that we may have life after death. I pray that this devotional study book has provided insight on how a Law Enforcement Officer can live out this life on duty as well as off duty. The Criminal Justice System can be a dark place, be salt and light.

ABOUT THE AUTHOR

Charles Gilliland has been in law enforcement for over twenty-two years. He started his career with the Dallas Police Department. After two years at Dallas he was hired by Dallas/Fort Worth International Airport Department of Public Safety. He spent his first year in the Anti-Air Piracy Division before being cross trained as a fire fighter. He worked two years as an Aircraft Crash Rescue Fire Fighter driving an Oshkosh M22 Crash truck. He transferred to the Patrol Division and worked to create DFW DPSs Bicycle Unit. In July of 2001 he promoted to Sergeant and returned to the Anti-Air Piracy Division. Today Charles currently serves as a Sergeant in the Patrol Division.

Charles serves as an Elder in his home church of Cottonwood Baptist Church in Dublin, Texas. He is a member of Gideon's International and enjoys any opportunity to share God's Word.

In 2005, Charles started a Law Enforcement Bible study in the Dallas Fort Worth area. The group quickly grew, leading Charles to seek out affiliation with The Fellowship of Christian Peace Officers (FCPO), a National Christian Law Enforcement Organization. In 2009 Charles was asked to serve on the National Board of Directors for FCPO.

Charles lives in the Dublin area with his wife Angie and their children Kate and Cole. Charles and Angie recently celebrated twenty years of marriage.

ThroughTheEyesOfaCop@gmail.com

If you are interested in becoming part of a
Christian Law Enforcement organization,
I would encourage you to visit www.FCPO.org.

CPSIA information can be obtained at www.ICGtesting.com
Printed in the USA
LVOW060602190712

290596LV00002B/1/P